FITTING

SOLUTIONS

FITTING
SOLUTIONS

PATTERN-ALTERING TIPS
FOR GARMENTS THAT FIT

The Taunton Press

Cover photo: Susan Kahn
Designer/Layout Artist: Amy L. Bernard

Typeface: Goudy
Paper: S. D. Warren, Somerset Matte, 70 lb.
Printer: Quebecor Printing, Kingsport, Tennessee

Taunton
BOOKS & VIDEOS

for fellow enthusiasts

First printing: February 1996
Second printing: June 1996
Printed in the United States of America

A THREADS Book

THREADS magazine® is a trademark of The Taunton Press, Inc.
registered in the U.S. Patent and Trademark Office.

The Taunton Press, 63 South Main Street, Box 5506,
Newtown, CT 06470-5506

Library of Congress Cataloging-in-Publication Data

Fitting solutions : pattern-altering tips for garments that fit.
        p. cm.
    "A Threads book"—T.p. verso.
    Selections from the Fitting column in Threads magazine, 1991-1995.
    Includes index.
    ISBN 1-56158-110-0
    1. Dressmaking—Pattern design. 2. Clothing and dress measurements.
I. Threads magazine.
TT520.F567 1996
646.4`07—dc20   95-45723
                                   CIP

CONTENTS

Chapter 3

THE BUST

Chapter 4

FROM THE WAIST DOWN

INTRODUCTION

Making clothes that really fit is one of garment making's greatest challenges—and crucial to success. No matter how lovely the fabric, how fine the garment design, or how expertly we sew, the results are disappointing if the garment fits poorly. The Fitting column in Threads magazine brings together fitting problems experienced by our readers and solutions provided by experts in fitting and pattern alteration.

In this volume are compiled the best of those dialogues from 1991 to 1995. The entries are organized by major areas of the body, and an index makes it easy to find what you need.

Nearly everyone has some kind of fitting challenge. You're sure to recognize a number of the fitting difficulties discussed, and the solutions presented will help you achieve that most important goal, clothes that fit well and look good.

For their contributions to this column, we thank Della Steineckert, associate professor in clothing and textiles at Brigham Young University, and coauthor, along with Elizabeth Liechty and Judith Rasband, of Fitting and Pattern Alteration: A Multi-Method Approach (Fairchild Publishing, 1986); Margaret Komives, clothing construction teacher at Milwaukee Area Technical College; Joyce Gale, instructor in pattern making and fitting at the Los Angeles Trade-Technical College; Britta Callamaras, teacher of pattern making who also fits and alters clothing; Dee DuMont, who fits and alters clothing on Bainbridge Island, WA; Elaine Rutledge, who conducts fitting clinics in Chunchula, AL; Cecelia Podolak, a clothing specialist who teaches at the University of British Columbia; and Jeltje Matheys, teacher of sewing and flat pattern design in Port Hope, ON, Canada.

—Mary Galpin Barnes, editor

Chapter 1

the
WHOLE FIGURE

CHOOSING A PATTERN WISELY

How can I tell by looking at a pattern if I'll have a fitting problem?
—Many readers

Margaret Komives advises:

It is very difficult to recognize fitting problems just by looking at patterns. I have been fitting adults for more than 20 years and can recognize only three such areas: a too-narrow sleeve cap, a shallow back-crotch curve in pants, and sloping shoulders.

If you buy your patterns by bust measurement and are having difficulties, try using your "high bust" measurement rather than the full bust. Take the tape measure under your arms and over the upper part of the bust. The garment will fit the neck and shoulders, and you can make bust adjustments.

Cecelia Podolak recommends:

To pretest the fit of a jacket pattern, cut and have a helper pin-fit the garment tissue before cutting the garment fabric. Wear a garment that might be worn under the jacket—a blouse or sweater. Pin shoulder pads in place; you may have to experiment to get the right pad. Pin the front and back tissues together at the shoulder seamline. All pins should be parallel to the seamlines, like large, metal basting stitches. Anchor the pattern to the blouse at the top of the center front (CF) and center back (CB) with pins, checking that the verticals align visually with the center of the body. All the darts should be pinned in place. Pin the underarm side seamline. Turn and pin the hem, and clip the neck and armhole curves so they lie flat on the body. Pin the sleeve together at the underarm seam, and to the bodice, but only from notch to notch (drawing top right). Pin the sleeve hem in place. Working from the top down to maintain the natural hang of the garment, check the following areas:

Pin-fitting a tissue

Begin at shoulder seam, then anchor CF and CB. Pin darts and side seam; pin sleeve at underarm.

Correcting excess back length

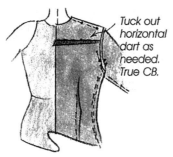

Tuck out horizontal dart as needed. True CB.

Correcting gape at neckline

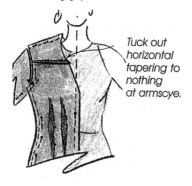

Tuck out horizontal tapering to nothing at armscye.

1. Shoulder length: A slightly extended shoulder (1½ in. past the shoulder point) will give the jacket and figure a better appearance.

2. Bust and hip circumference: A diagonal wrinkle will appear if the jacket is too snug in either the bust or the hips. Side seams can safely be let out ½ in. to ⅝ in., in which case the sleeve underarm should also be let out a corresponding amount, tapering to the wrist.

3. Back neck: A horizontal wrinkle may occur because of excess length. A small horizontal tuck at center back, tapering to nothing at the armhole (drawing above left), will correct the problem. Straighten the center-back seam after this correction is made.

4. Darts: Horizontal darts should angle upward and end approximately 1 in. from the bust point. Vertical darts may be directed to the bust point or set slightly to the side and may end ½ in. from the bust point. Adjust the pins and tucks as needed.

5. Side seams and back vent: If you have a swayback, the side seamlines may swing forward, and the vent may pull apart. A horizontal tuck of the pattern in the waist area from center back to nothing at the side seam will allow the side seam to hang straight. Straighten center-back seam.

6. Front chest: A cardigan neck may gape if there is excess pattern length between the shoulder and bust area. A horizontal tuck between the bust and shoulder tapering to nothing at the armhole will correct this (drawing below left). True the cardigan neckline after this correction is made, and make the same correction on the facing.

7. Waist: Pattern waistline markings should coincide with the body waistline, particularly if the garment has waist shaping. Lengthen or shorten the pattern between the bust and waist on the jacket front, back, and facing.

8. Sleeve circumference and length: There should be sufficient wearing ease in both the upper and lower arm. See p. 63 on adding ease to the sleeve. I prefer the sleeve to end just below the wrist bone.

9. Miscellaneous details: Check pocket size and placement, jacket length, and button placement.

ADJUSTING PATTERNS FOR HEIGHT

I'm 6 ft. tall and I have trouble deciding just where to add the extra length I need in clothes. Should a fraction of the length I would add to a skirt be added to the bottom of a blazer? And how do I determine the position of a pocket on a blazer or skirt? When repositioning buttons, should a larger button be used, or another one be added?
—Patt McDade, Chesterfield, MO

Della Steineckert replies:
Misses patterns are proportioned for a figure that is 5 ft. 5 in. to 5 ft. 6 in. tall. If you are taller (or shorter), naturally your pattern must be made longer (or shorter) too. And even if the total length of a pattern is correct, its distribution of length can be incorrect for your body. Thus, concepts regarding pattern length apply to us all.

Body length can vary proportionately or disproportionately in several areas. You first need to determine where your figure is longer compared to patterns. Pattern size charts provide only the center-back length from neck to waist; there are no general body-length guidelines. The best way to determine where your body length deviates from a pattern company's standards is to analyze the fit of clothes you've made from patterns by working through the following analysis. Refer to the drawing below.

If the waistline seam, elastic casing, etc., of dresses consistently rises above your belt (assuming a belt that rides at your natural waistline), the distance between the waistline seam and the bottom edge of the belt will

Pattern adjustments for body length

Variations in body length require corresponding changes to patterns. The location of the adjustments depends upon your body's proportions in the areas defined by the alteration lines.

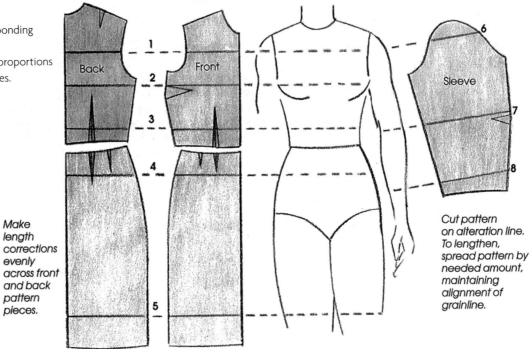

Back

Front

Sleeve

Make length corrections evenly across front and back pattern pieces.

Cut pattern on alteration line. To lengthen, spread pattern by needed amount, maintaining alignment of grainline.

indicate the overall additional bodice length needed. To determine where on your upper torso the additional length occurs, check the following:

If the armscye base cuts under the arm and wrinkles point toward the neck, either your upper rib cage or just the distance from shoulder to armpit is longer than average; you need to lengthen your patterns through the armscye (alteration line 1 on the drawing) and equally across the upper sleeve cap (line 6) just enough so that the armscye is comfortable. This alteration will lower the bust darts (or princess shaping) and the back-waist darts, and it will increase the depth of a low neckline. Then if more length is needed in the bodice, lengthen the pattern also near the waist (line 3).

If the armscye fits okay, but the bust and shoulder-blade shaping are consistently too high (bust darts are higher than your bust, back-waist darts reach to or above your shoulder blade), you need to lengthen bodice patterns below the armscye base but above the bust and shoulder-blade shaping (line 2); then add any additional needed length near the waist (line 3).

If both those upper bodice areas usually fit, lengthen the pattern entirely near the waist (line 3).

If sleeves are consistently too short, first check, and if necessary, correct tightness of the armscye as explained; lengthening the sleeve cap will lengthen the sleeve.

Next check the position of the elbow dart or shaping. Bend both elbows at once to form right angles near the waist. If the elbow dart tip or the center of the eased or curved area always falls above your elbow, lengthen sleeve patterns evenly above the elbow (line 7) until the shaping is at your elbow level; then lengthen the pattern additionally near the wrist (line 8) if necessary.

If the elbow shaping is generally correctly placed, or if the sleeve is a straight or flared style, lengthen the pattern entirely near the wrist (line 8).

On skirts and pants, side seam or buttocks shaping that consistently lies above your hip curvature indicates a long lower torso (waist to crotch). Lengthen the pattern below the front darts but through the back darts (line 4) as much as is necessary to position the shaping correctly; then add any remaining length you need near the hem (line 5).

If the hip and buttocks shaping of skirts is generally correctly placed, lengthen the skirt near the hem only.

For pants, if the crotch consistently cuts, and, on loose-fitting pants, if V-shaped wrinkles form from the crotch to the side waistline, the crotch depth of pants patterns is too short for you. Lengthen the pattern below the front darts but through the back darts (line 4) as explained earlier.

Once you identify where your body is consistently longer than the pattern standards, you'll know where to make corrections to future patterns, whether or not they have identifiable landmarks such as back-waist darts or bust darts.

Joyce Gale adds:

Rather than examining finished garments for proportions, you can measure the pattern and compare it to your body measurements, then make corrections as needed to position shaping devices such as bust darts or curved side seams at the hip, at your body's curvature. The basic body measurements you'll need are shoulder-to-bust point, center-back waist length, waist to largest part of hip, and waist to desired hem. After you've made any length adjustments, cut a trial garment in muslin and try it on. This is the only way to tell if garment proportions or style lines need to be altered.

Also, when you need to elongate a pattern, consider the style of the garment. In general, if it's loose-fitting and has an unfitted sleeve, such as a dolman-type sleeve or a dropped shoulder, you can simply add the extra length to the hem and/or sleeves, even if it's your torso, not your legs, that is extra long.

Margaret Komives talks about pleasing proportions:

When you need to change the length of a garment because you are taller (or shorter) than average, you must consider what length will create the most pleasing proportions for your height. The basic guideline is that no horizontal line should cut your figure in half.

Start by establishing skirt length, because so much depends on it. Skirt length depends in turn on the shape of the legs. Can the skirt end just above the calf, or would a below-the-calf length be more attractive? (A hemline should never fall at the fullest part of the calf.) Are your legs attractive enough that the hem can be at, just below, or even above the knee?

Once you've determined skirt length, evaluate blazer length. Wearing a similar skirt of the right length, don the jacket. The jacket hemline should fall either above or below the halfway point between skirt hemline and shoulder line, but not at the fullest part of the hip. In general, full skirts look best with shorter jackets, slim skirts with longer jackets.

You might find it helpful to visit a store specializing in ready-made clothing for tall people. Analyze the lengths and proportions of the clothes that look good on you (take along a tape measure).

As for darts, if you lengthen a jacket at the lengthen/shorten line on the pattern, which is usually through the midriff, the darts should be lengthened correctly. Again, however, a lot depends on your own figure—darts should end just short of the relevant apex (hip bone, bust point, etc.). Pin or baste the dart, then try on the garment. You often need to adjust the width or length of darts as a result of a try-on.

As for pockets, if you lengthen a jacket, you should lower the pockets in order to maintain the jacket's style lines. Lengthening a jacket at the pattern's lengthen/shorten line will automatically reposition the pockets. But a pocket shouldn't be so low that your hand doesn't reach the bottom. And the pockets of coats should not be positioned so as to halve the figure. When evaluating pocket position, always turn up the hem to its correct height and wear the shoes and hose you'll wear with the garment (even hose color can affect the appearance).

When lengthening a jacket, you can either add another button or increase the distance between buttons. If you lengthen the distance between buttons, a slightly larger button may be warranted. To determine button size, I have my students cut paper circles the size and color of the intended button and pin them to the jacket or coat.

If you use a larger button than specified, you should increase the distance between the button and the edge of the coat, still maintaining the center-front line. Just sew a narrower seam at the front edge.

BIG ON TOP, SMALL ON THE BOTTOM

I'm a rather novice sewer and my problem is that I'm two completely different sizes: 18 to 20 in waist and top, and 12 in hips and legs. I hope you can find ideas on how to hide my tummy.
—Bette Byers, Oakland, CA

Dee DuMont replies:
Big size differences between top and bottom do make for big fitting headaches, but there are remedies. When choosing fashions to sew, select separates. The stylish new look of a long tunic (or sweater) over tapered pants would show off those slim legs. Consider garments that avoid fitted waistlines—jumpers and dropped-waist dresses, for example.

Sometimes the waistline measurement indicates a size 18 to 20 pattern but the rest of you really doesn't warrant such a large size. When buying patterns that cover both the top and the bottom, select the pattern size for the bust (and upper torso) area, and alter for the waist and hips, since those are much simpler pattern adjustments.

Assuming your waist—particularly the tummy—is large in relation to the hip and leg, let's alter pants. If you don't want to change the hipline, increase the waist by making a diagonal slash from the waist seam down to the hip area and spreading the pattern at the waist, as shown in the drawing above left. This can be done on both the front and back pattern pieces, or only in the front if the problem is primarily in the abdominal area.

Slash to—but not through—hip and spread to add to waist.

Slash to—but not through— hip and spread to lengthen crotch seam.

In addition to a waist increase, a full tummy can also require an increase in the length of the center front seam of the pants to allow the garment to fit to the waist. To find your length from the inseam to the waist, tie a washer or other weight in the middle of a yard of string. Put the string between your legs, placing the washer at the inseam point of the crotch. Gently pull both ends of the string up to your waistline. Mark the string where it crosses the waistline, front and back. Remove the string and measure. Usually the back is longer, but a full tummy and a flat fanny can reverse this ratio.

Make a slash on the pattern from the center front to—but not through—the side seam, beginning above the curve of the center front seam. Then spread the pattern until it matches your measurement, as shown in the drawing above right.

You can use this procedure to reduce excess fullness by overlapping rather than spreading the pattern.

Redrawing the grainline of a modified pattern

Unadjusted pattern

CB

Original grainline tilts from waist to neck.

New grainline is perpendicular to the floor.

Slash along waist from CB up to side seam. Overlap skirt ¾ in. in CB; taper to nothing at side seam.

Grainline is parallel to CB

Bodice CB is on bias.

Redraw dart symmetrical to the dart center line.

Skirt CB is on grain.

Elaine Rutledge adds:

Here's a way to lengthen the crotch for a big tummy that will not throw the dart off grain. Slash down a grainline on one side of the dart to the point where the bottom of the tummy starts protruding. Slash from that point on a cross-grain line through the center front. Spread out and up as required by the individual's measurements and true the seamlines. Chances are the dart must be altered as well, usually to be shorter and less deep at the waist.

ADJUSTING FOR SHORT BACK WAIST

Several years ago, I was measured for a basic pattern and discovered that I am ½ in. shorter in the back from waistline to hipline than most patterns. This explains the trouble my mother had sewing for me as a child and why all my clothes wanted to hang lower in the back.

I wear a lot of dresses. Even though I know what the problem is, I've never been able to correct patterns satisfactorily. I was instructed to make a ½-in. fold at the center back of the pattern about 2 in. below the waistline then taper the fold across the pattern to nothing at the side seams. That seems to remove the extra fullness but leaves me with a hemline that is off grain.
—Mary W. Fuller, Alexandria, VA

Joyce Gale replies:

The instructions you have received are essentially correct, but I would adjust the pattern as shown in the drawing at left. Perhaps you also need to correct the grain placement. In a one-piece pattern, it is impossible to keep the entire center back of an adjusted pattern on grain. The best solution for this would be to place the grainline as shown. This will keep your hemline at right angles to the center-back skirt and on grain. The center-back bodice will be slightly off grain, but this is not really going to give you any problems as long as you're cutting the garment in a solid-colored fabric.

If you want to use a plaid fabric, it would be better to put a seam at the waistline so that both the center-back bodice and center-back skirt could be placed on the straight grain.

Jeltje Matheys further comments:

First convert the dress back to a basic princess line by extending the dart lines to the shoulder seam and hem. On the center-back pattern, fold 1½ in. from the bodice along the waistline, as shown in the drawing above right. On the side-back pattern piece, fold 1½ in. at the princess seamline only, tapering to nothing at the side seam. For cutting, you can place the center-back section on the fold.

Draw a new grainline on the side panel as shown. The upper portion of the side panel will be somewhat on the bias. Or curve the princess seam to the armscye and leave the upper portion of the side panel as part of the center-back section, where it will be more on grain.

Elizabeth Liechty and Judith Rasband suggest:

This method keeps the center back on grain. Pattern shortening is done at the neck and shoulder seamlines, so the garment is lifted into position.

Start by cutting the pattern barely below the seamline along the neck and shoulder, releasing the seam allowance (see the drawing below right). Clip into—but not through—the seam allowance at the neck and shoulder corners, dart center, and at the most curved part of the neck. The allowance will pivot at the clip points, allowing it to lie flat during the maneuvers that follow.

Converting a one-piece pattern to a princess line
(To correct for a short back waist)

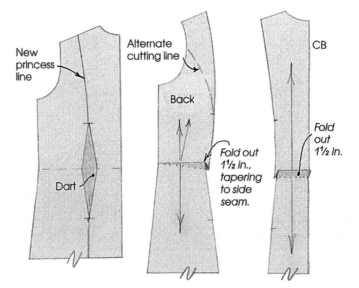

New princess line

Alternate cutting line

CB

Back

Fold out 1½ in.

Dart

Fold out 1½ in., tapering to side seam.

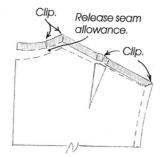

Clip.

Release seam allowance.

Clip.

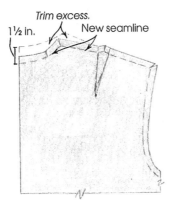

Trim excess.
1½ in.
New seamline

Lower the neck seam allowance at the center back the amount of excess back-waist length (drawing left). You must keep the allowance perpendicular to the center back or a dip will form at center back in the final pattern. The clip in the neck curve will close and overlap, creating a tighter curve, but the neck circumference remains the same. The clips at the neck and shoulder corners will spread. The clip at the dart will overlap slightly. Tape the allowance in place, and trim excess tissue from outside the seam allowance. Restore the dart length. The pattern is now ready to use.

FITTING FOR THE MATURE FIGURE

Please address the fitting concerns of aging sewers, who find that gravity has lowered bustlines and hiplines and that new bumps have appeared.
—Pauline Bruss, Milwaukee, WI

Della Steineckert replies:

Like it or not, when age 50 creeps up, middle-age "maturity" begins to settle in. Gravity seems to work overtime as bulges blossom in formerly flat areas, and bone, muscle, and fatty tissue rearrange themselves. In order to counterbalance the redistribution of weight, posture, too, changes.

Each category of physical change requires a corresponding type of pattern adjustment. Following are general rules. When an indented area (such as the waist) thickens, width needs to be added by letting out the darts (side-seam shaping at the waist is also a dart). Where a bulge (such as the buttocks) flattens, the pattern needs to be shortened at its upper edge, width removed along the side or center, and the darts narrowed to restore the seamline length. Where bulges develop or enlarge (such as a protruding abdomen), the edge of the pattern area above the bulge needs to be lengthened, width added at the side or center, and the darts widened at the upper edge to create more depth and restore seamline lengths.

The most common changes that occur on the mature figure and the pattern changes called for are described below. To determine the alterations you need, I suggest working with a fitting pattern and analyzing its fit as described below. Your fashion patterns will not always require alterations at each area in which your body has changed. For example, even if your waist has thickened, a shift dress (no waistline seam) won't require a waistline alteration; even if your bust has lowered, a dartless bodice won't require that you reposition the bust shaping. Numbers in the text refer to steps in the drawings.

Rounded upper back—The curvature of the upper spine increases, the head tilts forward, and the chest compresses.

Effect on garment—The back bodice pulls upward toward the curvature. At center back, waistline and hem ride up. On the front, the neckline pulls up and chafes the neck. Fabric sags at the chest. Center-front edges, pleats, slits, and vents flare open at the hem, which hangs low.

Pattern adjustment (drawing right)—

1. Add length just below the back neckline, tapering to the armscye.

2. Transfer the back-shoulder dart to the center back at the shoulder blade line to add further length over the curvature, then create a neckline dart, letting it absorb some extra length to straighten the center-back edge.

3. Add width evenly along center back, then widen waistline and neckline darts to absorb the extra width and maintain neckline and waistline lengths.

4. At center front, shorten the chest area by lowering the neckline, tapering to nothing at the armscye.

General compression—Bone mass diminishes and spinal discs flatten. Height decreases both above and below the waist.

Effect on garments—The bodice droops above the waistline; hip shaping falls below the hip curvature. The crotch hangs low.

Alteration for a rounded upper back*

*Clip seam allowances as necessary to maintain flat pattern edges and smooth curves. True stitching and cutting lines.

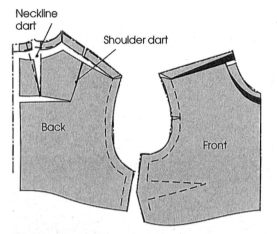

1. Release and raise seam allowance at neckline and shoulder.

2. Slash from CB to tip of shoulder dart; slash and close shoulder dart. Slash down from neckline and spread to straighten CB line.

3. Add width at CB. Widen neckline and waistline dart.

4. Release seam allowance at front neckline and shoulder; overlap to shorten.

Pattern adjustment—Shorten back and front bodice patterns evenly above but near the waist, skirt or pants patterns below the waist. If you also have a rounded upper back, there may appear to be no excess fabric at the waist because your upper back has borrowed it; once you add length to the upper back, the excess will reappear near the waistline and need to be corrected.

Rounded shoulders—The shoulder ball joint and collar bones move forward.

Alteration for rounded shoulders*

*Clip seam allowances as necessary to maintain flat pattern edges and smooth curves. True stitching and cutting lines.

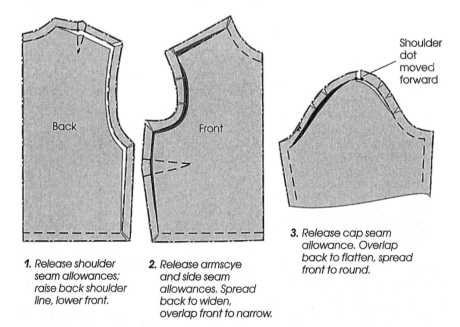

Shoulder dot moved forward

1. Release shoulder seam allowances; raise back shoulder line, lower front.

2. Release armscye and side seam allowances. Spread back to widen, overlap front to narrow.

3. Release cap seam allowance. Overlap back to flatten, spread front to round.

Effect on garments—At the armscye, the shoulder seam lies behind the crest of the shoulders. Front armscyes seem too small because they cut against the joint. Back armscyes and sleeves pull to the back; back sleeve areas hang loose and appear large.

Pattern adjustment (drawing on p. 16)—

1. Raise the shoulder seam on the back bodice and lower it by an equivalent amount on the front, tapering to nothing at the neckline. Move the shoulder dot on the sleeve cap toward the front by the amount of adjustment.

2. Add width evenly along back armscye, tapering to nothing near the waistline. Decrease width along the front armscye at chest level only, tapering to nothing at the waistline and adding at the shoulder to match the back-width increase.

3. Shape the sleeve cap curves back and front.

Lowered bustline—Bust tissue becomes pendulous and the bustline lowers.

Effect on garment—Dart tips and other shaping details lie above the bust. Bodices pull tight across bust fullness, and center closures gap.

Pattern adjustment—Reposition front darts or other shaping details to correspond to your bustline level. If there are waistline darts, you can leave them unstitched and gather the fullness at the waistline. Or release the darts for a looser waistline, adding equivalent width to the skirt waistline; wear a belt for shaping.

Thickened waist—Waistline thickens at sides and/or midriff, reducing the degree of waistline indentation.

Effect on garment—Fitted clothing pulls into the soft waistline tissue. Center-front closures gape. Belts and waistbands crumple.

Pattern alteration—Add width to the sides at the waistline: Cut within the garment area alongside the side seamline, dipping at the hip, then spread at the waistline, tapering to nothing at armscye and hip level. Let out front waistline darts. Adjust waistband quarters to correspond.

Broadened hips—Hip curvature becomes fuller.

Effect on garment—Skirts and pants pull across the hipline, loose pleats pull open, and side pockets gape. Skirts ride up around the torso, forming a fold below the waist.

Pattern alteration—Widen skirt patterns evenly from the hemline to the hip, by cutting alongside the side stitching line within the garment area and spreading the pattern; taper to nothing at the waistline. Clip seam allowances as necessary. On pants patterns taper the width back to nothing near the knee.

Flattened buttocks, enlarged abdomen (drawing on p. 19)—Buttocks muscles flatten and the abdomen enlarges and protrudes. These changes usually happen in tandem.

Effect on garment—Back hems hang low and rest against the legs. Waistline and hemline ride up at center front, and the entire front of skirts or pants pulls upward toward the abdomen. On fitted skirts, the back pulls forward. Side seams curve forward at the hem. The back crotch pulls into the body; front crotch and inseam may be forced too low and form a fold at the crotch.

Pattern alteration—For the flattened buttocks:

1. Shorten skirts and pants evenly across the center back near the waist, tapering to nothing at the side seam.

2. Narrow the back darts and restore their length.

3. Remove width evenly along the center-back seam or fold line and, on pants, at the crotch tip, taper to nothing at the knee.

For the enlarged abdomen:

4. Lengthen skirts and pants across center front near the waist, tapering to nothing at the side seam; restore length of darts. If necessary, also add

Alteration for flattened buttocks, enlarged abdomen*

*Clip seam allowances as necessary to maintain flat pattern edges and smooth curves. True stitching and cutting lines.

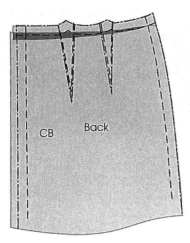

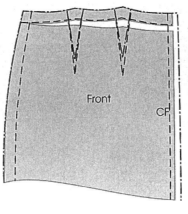

1. Cut below waist seamline; overlap to shorten.

2. Redraw back darts narrower and restore length.

3. Redraw CB seam to remove width.

4. Raise seam allowances to add length at CF. Restore dart length.

width at center front evenly from waist to hem; widen darts to maintain waist size.

On pants, widen front crotch extensions, tapering to nothing near the knee. Deepen the curve of the back crotch and lift and flatten the curve of the front crotch.

Enlarged buttocks—The pattern alterations for an enlarged abdomen (p. 18) apply to the back skirt and pant patterns. If the back has only one dart, move the dart slightly toward center back and transfer part of its width into a new dart toward the side, forming a two-dart pattern.

ASYMMETRIC BODIES

Could your experts provide some general clothing guidelines for fitting a person with a curved spine? Nothing about me is symmetrical. Wearing a shoulder pad on my low shoulder does not begin to solve the problem.
—Susan Lamons, Daytona Beach, FL

Margaret Komives replies:
Two styles that I have found to be very flattering on the person with a curved spine are the blouson and the shirt dress, both shown in the drawing at left. You should avoid anything with horizontal and vertical lines (plaids, stripes, checks) as well as garments with a waistline seam. Outside of adjusting the height of shoulder pads, nothing can be done to the shoulder to disguise it. It can be fitted by lowering the shoulder of the bodice on the side that needs it (drawing on p. 21). The sleeve pattern won't need any adjustment since the armscye has not changed.

Styles that disguise a curved spine

Blouson top

Shirt dress

Dee DuMont replies:

Garments that hang from the shoulder are the most flattering and require minimal fitting, while separates tend to accentuate physical misalignments, such as one hip being higher than the other. Closely fitting a garment to an imbalanced body can often draw attention to the irregularities, and except in extreme cases, it is not recommended.

It does sound like you want to want to wear fitted clothing, so I suggest that you make a four-part pattern, especially for the bodice area. Alter each quadrant—left and right fronts and backs—separately to fit, and then join the pattern pieces at center front and center back. If your garment has a center-back closure, make it perpendicular to the ground, rather than following your spine.

Adjustment for a low shoulder

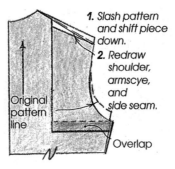

1. Slash pattern and shift piece down.
2. Redraw shoulder, armscye, and side seam.

Original pattern line

Overlap

Chapter 2
✤

NECK,
SHOULDERS &
ARMS

FITTING A JEWEL NECKLINE

I do not know how to fit a jewel neckline or Peter Pan collar for my thin neck. Please help.
—Mary Elassman, Loma Linda, CA

Della Steineckert replies:

The basic process for fitting a jewel neckline is the same whether your neck is thin, thick, or in between. The pattern neckline is made smaller in circumference for a thin neck, larger for a heavy neck. The neck opening should never be made smaller or larger by taking in or letting out the center-front, center-back, or shoulder seams—this would create utter havoc with fit everywhere!

A jewel neckline sits at the base of the neck. Likewise, a flat collar, such as the Peter Pan collar, lies flat over the chest, shoulders, and upper back; its neckline shape is a near duplicate of the bodice neckline curvature.

The back edge of a well-fitting jewel neckline crosses the middle of the vertebra at the neck, and the side and center-front edges lie slightly wider and lower than where the neck meets the shoulder and collarbone. One's head can be turned without chafing the neck cords. The fabric lies relaxed; closures fasten easily without stress or gaping.

I suggest making a muslin fitting yoke, 7 in. to 8 in. long at center front and center back, from a basic dress bodice pattern; have a friend help you fit it. The shoulders must fit properly because you cannot correct the neck unless they do. Place the yoke center front on the fold, and leave 1-in. seam allowances at center back and neck. Cut along the armscye and shoulder cutting lines. Mark the neck and center-back stitching lines. Stitch and press shoulder darts and seams and press under one seam allowance along center back.

To fit the yoke, first place a choker-length strand of small beads or a chain around your neck and adjust its length until it defines the jewel

Altering a jewel neckline and flat collar

Use a fitting yoke to fit neckline. Make same alterations to neckline of flat collar styles as to bodice neckline.

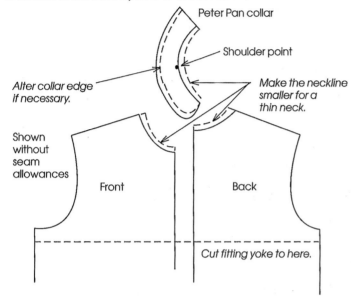

Peter Pan collar

Shoulder point

Alter collar edge if necessary.

Make the neckline smaller for a thin neck.

Shown without seam allowances

Front

Back

Cut fitting yoke to here.

neckline position you want. Put on the yoke over the chain, pinning at the center back and aligning the centers vertically with your body centers. The neck seam allowance edges will be tight and show grain distortion.

Have your friend clip the neck seam allowance at right angles to the edge, at ½-in. intervals, ending each clip at the chain. The clips will open as strain is relieved and will cease opening when the strain is eased. Remove the chain. Where the fabric still strains, extend each clip slightly. The back neckline may require fewer and shorter clips than the front. When the yoke fits your neck smoothly, remove the yoke.

Fold the yoke in half along the center-front line, matching the cut edges of left to right halves, and lay it flat. Draw a smooth neck stitching line connecting the ends of the clips, having the stitching line intersect center-front and -back lines at right angles. Trim the seam allowance to ⅝ in. Then pin the pattern pieces over the yoke, matching the original necklines. Cross out the pattern's original neck seamlines and trace your new neckline. Add seam allowances. Correct the stitching and cutting lines of facings as well.

Because the neckline shape of flat collar styles such as the Peter Pan collar are nearly the same as that of the bodice, you need to make approximately the same alteration to the collar neckline as you made to your jewel neckline. Measure the distance from the original to the new stitching line on your adjusted bodice pattern at center front, center back, and shoulder. Alter the neck stitching line of the collar by equivalent amounts, and redraw the collar neckline in a smooth curve (see drawing at left). Add seam allowances. If the proportions of the collar now seem off (the collar may be too wide if you've adjusted for a thin neck), you can decrease the width along the collar's outer edge equal to the neckline adjustment. Taper to zero where the collar's outer edge meets the neckline, so that the collar's neckline length does not change.

Margaret Komives adds hints for fitting yourself:

Start with a basic pattern; you will find one at the end of the dress section in most pattern catalogs. Cut the back bodice in one piece by laying the center-back seamline on the fold of the fabric. For the front, add a ⅝-in. seam allowance beyond the center-front fold line and place the cutting line along the selvage.

Cut the bodice from a nonraveling woven fabric or a soft nonwoven, such as Pellon 910. For a thin neck, add about ½ in. to the neckline seam allowance (making the neck circumference smaller). Machine-baste the shoulder and underarm seams together. Try on the garment and pin the center-front seam closed. While looking in a mirror, use a soft (No. 1) lead pencil to trace around the base of your neck.

Remove the shell and staystitch the neck edge following the pencil marks. Trim the seam allowance to about ½ in. and clip down to the staystitching all around the neckline. Try on the shell again. Mark corrections with a colored pencil and staystitch with a different color thread. Clip as needed. Transfer the new neckline to the basic pattern, taping tissue to the pattern if necessary.

An attractive way to finish a jewel neckline is to use a self-fabric binding instead of a facing. Keep in mind that unless the binding is turned completely toward the wrong side, the finished neckline edge will be smaller by the width of the binding. For knit fabrics, folding under the seam allowance and topstitching with a double needle is easy and gives a professional-looking finish.

MULTIPLE NECKLINE CORRECTIONS

After fruitless attempts to get blouses not to pull up and gather at the neck, I made up a basic fitting shell and discovered that I have square shoulders. But solving this problem revealed others. First, wrinkles form only in the front on the right side. Second, the fabric cuts into my neck on this side only, revealing an asymmetric neck. Cutting the neck larger doesn't eliminate the wrinkles; the blouse feels as though I need to pull the right shoulder toward the arm. Third, my head tilts forward, requiring the front neck to be lowered by ½ in., and I have a slight hump at the back of the neck. Do I add the same amount to the back of the neck?

After solving these fitting problems on the fitting shell, how do I apply the corrections to each new pattern without going to the expense of a trial muslin each time?

—Irene Gamble, Wildwood Crest, NJ

Della Steineckert responds:

As you observed, correcting one area of poor fit will often reveal other areas. And adjacent figure variations cause a chain reaction of wrinkles. To complicate matters, because a larger-than-average figure area pulls fabric from other areas, it can cause the appearance of additional figure variations and fitting problems that do not in fact exist.

To solve your fitting problems, first analyze how your figure variations affect your clothes. Always start with symmetric figure variations; work downward from the variation that is highest on your body.

You say you have already corrected for square shoulders, so I will address only the other areas. The fullness at the nape of your neck gives you a longer back length, pulling the back neck upward and the front along with it. The forward tilt of your neck amplifies these factors. The asymmetry at the right neck edge gives you additional body height and depth at this area and borrows ease from the armscye.

When correcting your basic pattern, first address the symmetric changes. The drawing on p. 28 shows the sequence of neck alterations to a basic pattern.

To accommodate back-neck fullness, raise the back neckline (A in drawing). To adjust for a forward-tilting neck, lower the front neckline (B). At the back, raise the neck point (the point where the neckline meets the shoulder seam) by only half the amount you lowered the front neckline, so as not to emphasize your neck's forward tilt.

To accommodate asymmetric right-neck fullness, raise the front and back neck points for the right side only (C). At center back, raise the neckline by only half the neck-point alteration to keep the back neckline as level as possible and deemphasize the asymmetry. To distinguish left from right when there are asymmetric fitting changes to a half pattern piece, I use red pencil for right-side markings, blue for left.

Now we get to the tricky part—your fashion patterns. First locate the essential pattern lines on the fashion pattern—center back, center front, shoulder line (indicated by a dot at the neckline and armscye if the shoulder seam is not at the natural shoulder line), base of fashion armscye, side seam (indicated by a dot at the base of the armscye and the hem if the garment has no side seam), and waistline.

Then, if the fashion pattern is the same brand, copyright issue, size, and figure type as your basic pattern, simply make the same fitting adjustments to the fashion pattern as you made to your basic pattern. This builds your personal measurement needs into the fashion pattern but retains the pattern's style, the styling details, and the design ease.

Even when the fashion pattern differs from your basic pattern in any one of the factors listed (a different pattern brand, for example), you can still achieve very good fit with the above approach because the slopers used by all the pattern companies are more alike than different. Simply cut generous seam allowances to allow for refining.

Adjusting for multiple neckline variations

When there are multiple corrections, make symmetric changes first, then asymmetric ones. (Shown without seam allowances.)

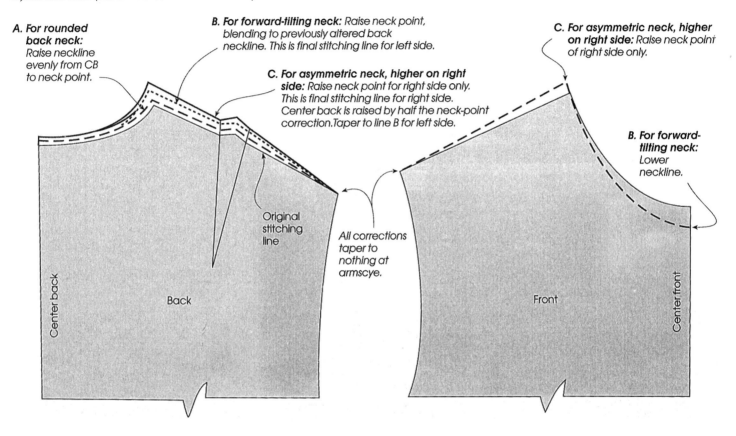

A. For rounded back neck: Raise neckline evenly from CB to neck point.

B. For forward-tilting neck: Raise neck point, blending to previously altered back neckline. This is final stitching line for left side.

C. For asymmetric neck, higher on right side: Raise neck point for right side only. This is final stitching line for right side. Center back is raised by half the neck-point correction. Taper to line B for left side.

C. For asymmetric neck, higher on right side: Raise neck point of right side only.

B. For forward-tilting neck: Lower neckline.

Original stitching line

All corrections taper to nothing at armscye.

Center back

Back

Front

Center front

When cutting out pattern pieces that have asymmetric alterations, cut both fabric layers on the outermost cutting line. Thread-trace the stitching lines for right and left sides through both fabric layers, using pink thread for the right side, blue for the left. Then simply stitch on the blue markings for left-side seamlines, on the pink for right-side seamlines.

SHORT, THICK NECK

In no book have I ever found a solution to fitting a short, thick neck. Even Sew-Fit patterns, when adjusted, ride my neck. Perhaps it's not the neck, but the shoulders? Whatever the cause of the problem, I've tossed out many a garment because I couldn't stand the pressure on the back of the neck.
—Shirley McCoy, Seattle, WA

Britta Callamaras advises:

If the garment rides up in the back neckline, most likely the problem is in fitting the shoulder area. If you can get Polaroid pictures of yourself, front, back, and sideways, without including your head, in underclothes only, you will probably be able to identity the problem right away. (We are so used to looking at faces that we tend to gloss over the rest of the body.) If you need more information, have someone take a picture of you wearing a garment that rides up, from the back view. Before it rides up, you'll probably see diagonal wrinkles pointing to the problem area. Wrinkles may point in another direction when the garment has ridden up, and this will give you an additional clue.

Correcting for a thick neck

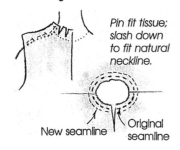

Pin fit tissue; slash down to fit natural neckline.

New seamline   Original seamline

Margaret Komives adds:

This problem is an easy one to explain but will need a few trials to correct. Very simply, cut the neckline larger by lowering the seamline (see drawing at left), then enlarge the collar or neckband. Cut the pattern as is, then put the garment on and determine whether it needs lowering in the front, back, or the same amount all the way around. Make changes in small increments, $\frac{1}{8}$ in. at a time. Measure the resulting neckline carefully by placing the tape measure on its side; add to the collar or neckband in corresponding amounts. A straight band can be added to at the centers, while a more curved collar can be enlarged by moving the neckline seam outward.

Joyce Gale suggests:

The most likely problem is that the neck opening is too small and too high in relation to the point where your neck meets your shoulder. You will need someone to help you, since this alteration is too difficult to do by yourself. Cut out your test bodice allowing an additional 1 in. at the top of each shoulder, starting at the neckline and tapering to nothing at the end of the shoulder. Sew the side seams together and put on the garment. Now smooth the garment over your chest so it lies perfectly flat, and pin it to your bra straps so it remains securely in place. Repeat the same procedure for the back. Now pin the shoulder seams together using as much of the extra allowance as needed. If the shoulder seams are not perfectly aligned, ignore that for the moment. Mark the neckline shape where it seems comfortable to you. Follow the line established by a necklace for a nice rounded shape. Mark the new seamline, including the shoulder point, on both the front and back pieces. Most shoulder seams are straight lines, but if your shoulder silhouette is more curved, there is no reason not to make your shoulder seams curved also (see drawing at right). Now true the shoulder seams by adding to or trimming either the front or the back armscye as needed. All these changes can be made to future patterns, but check first, since all pattern companies do not use the same basic patterns.

Dee DuMont adds:

While men's shirts are sized by neck circumference, women's are not. It took me years to figure out that I had a large neck in relation to my pattern size, and if I simply increased the center back by an inch, everything would fit just fine. (I also had to change the facing and the collar patterns.) I did not need longer shoulder seams, but I did need more room at the base of the neck in the back as well as across the upper shoulder. The change can be made all the way from neckline to hem, or the slash can go to—but not through—the waistline, and the pattern spread at the slash.

SHOULDER-PAD ALTERATIONS

I have very narrow, square, forward-thrust shoulders. How can I make or modify shoulder pads so they extend the necessary width without adding much to the height in the front, but will still fill in the hollow in the back?
—*Dorcas Watkins, Flushing, MI*

Della Steineckert replies:

Shoulder pads are by far the easiest and least expensive way to "correct" shoulder variations. With properly designed, custom shoulder pads, sloping shoulders can appear straight, uneven shoulders can be leveled, and narrow shoulders can be widened. Pads can also recontour the shoulders—they can round flat areas, fill in and smooth figure hollows, and

Alternative for a thick neck

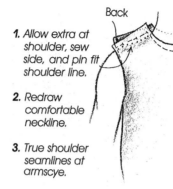

1. Allow extra at shoulder, sew side, and pin fit shoulder line.

2. Redraw comfortable neckline.

3. True shoulder seamlines at armscye.

smooth bony protrusions (in the last case, the underneath layers of padding are reamed out to create a hollow, allowing the pads to settle over the bony bumps instead of sitting on top of them).

To take full advantage of the potential of shoulder pads, first analyze the shoulder contour and its relation to the rest of the body (see drawings on facing page). An easy way to analyze the front and sides of the figure involves marking a full-length mirror with vertical and horizontal reference lines. To do this, first center a string vertically from the top to the bottom of the mirror and tape it taut. Evenly space another vertical string on each side of the first one, approximately at armscye width (even with the creases between the arm and rib cage). Then tape four horizontal strings parallel to the floor: one at shoulder/neck height, one about $1\frac{1}{2}$ in. below this to check the shoulder pitch, one at waistline level, and one at hip level.

As an alternative to using a mirror, you can have a friend help you take figure photos, which will let you evaluate the back view as well and see your side view without turning your head. Photos also give you a permanent record that you can use repeatedly. For a background, mark a wide piece of white or colored paper as described for the mirror, and tape it to a door. Stand in front of the background while the photos are taken, and for each shot, align the center of the body with the center line on the paper.

With either method, analyze the width, height, and slope of each shoulder from the front, noting any differences between left and right sides. From each side, look at your shoulder-joint positioning and posture. Compare your figure to the shoulder contours shown in the drawing at right.

With either method, dress in well-fitted underwear or a one-piece swimsuit or leotard worn over a well-fitted bra. With the photo method, your clothing should contrast with the paper color. In both cases, pin your hair up off your neck. Relax, stand normally with your hands hanging naturally at your sides, and look straight ahead.

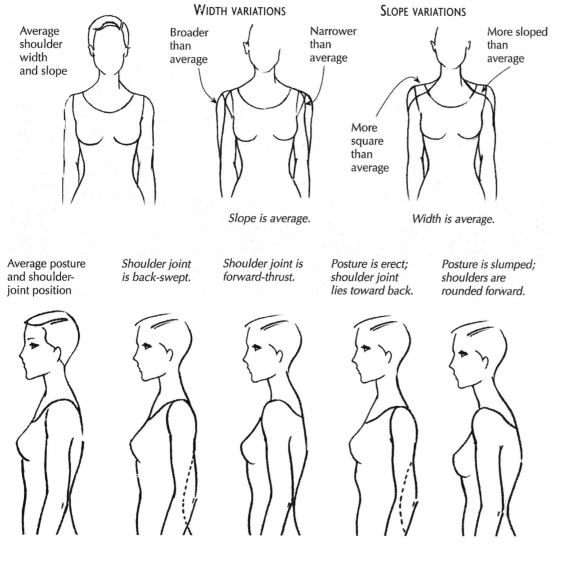

WIDTH VARIATIONS

Average shoulder width and slope

Broader than average

Narrower than average

SLOPE VARIATIONS

More sloped than average

More square than average

Slope is average.

Width is average.

Shoulder contours and positions

Compare each of your shoulders with the figures shown here. Keep in mind that multiple variations and asymmetrical shoulders are quite common.

Average posture and shoulder-joint position

Shoulder joint is back-swept.

Shoulder joint is forward-thrust.

Posture is erect; shoulder joint lies toward back.

Posture is slumped; shoulders are rounded forward.

For the side-view analysis using a mirror, you'll have to turn your head toward the mirror. And remember that with this method, your figure is in mirror image, so record your observations accurately (hold a pencil or small object in your right hand to make sure you don't get confused).

You may find that your shoulders are symmetrical (that is, alike on left and right) or asymmetrical, with one side higher or lower, more or less forward, or flatter or more protruding than the other. You may find one side average in some respects and the other not. If your figure is asymmetrical, definitely use shoulder pads to even the shoulders.

After analyzing your shoulder contours and position, you can determine how to use shoulder pads to make any needed visual corrections. For example, for a shoulder that slopes more than average, simply use a pad thicker than the pattern calls for. How much thicker depends on how sloped your shoulder is.

In your case, since your shoulders are narrower, squarer, and more forward-thrust than average, you need to add thickness only to the back of the shoulders to compensate for the forward thrust (no extra is needed on top of your shoulder). The easiest way to do this is to rotate the pad toward the back. This puts the thickest part of the pad (the top) slightly to the back where needed, while at the same time slightly reducing the thickness of the pad at the top of the shoulder.

Here's how to do it: Use standard pads (with an evenly cut, straight outer edge) that extend slightly beyond the armscye line and that are made with layers of fleece (you can't do this with molded pads). Flatten one of the pads and trace around it to make a pattern. Mark the shoulder line on the pattern (the armscye and neck edges of shoulder pads are usually clipped at the shoulder line). Slash the pattern just to the back of the shoulder line, and spread the pattern by 1 in. to 2 in., as shown in the drawing on facing page. Add ½ in. to the back edge. If you also have a hollow above the bust, which often accompanies forward-thrust shoulders, square the front of the pattern, as shown.

Customizing shoulder pads for rounded square shoulders

Adding a fleece cover to a pad allows the pad to be rotated to the back, putting extra fullness at the back while reducing height at the top of the shoulders.

MAKING PATTERN FOR A FLEECE COVER

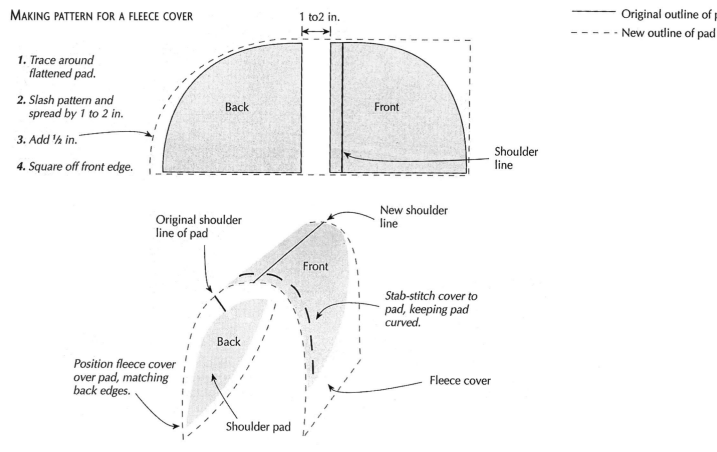

1 to 2 in.

1. Trace around flattened pad.

2. Slash pattern and spread by 1 to 2 in.

3. Add ½ in.

4. Square off front edge.

Back

Front

Shoulder line

—————— Original outline of pad

– – – – – New outline of pad

Original shoulder line of pad

New shoulder line

Front

Back

Stab-stitch cover to pad, keeping pad curved.

Position fleece cover over pad, matching back edges.

Shoulder pad

Fleece cover

Use this pattern to make a cover for your shoulder pads, cutting it from a felt or fleece fabric such as Thermolam, available from most fabric stores. For a crisper look, you can make an additional covering from a heavyweight, stable nonwoven such as Pellon. Stabstitch the cover(s) over the top of the original pad, matching the back of the pad with the back of the cover (the cover will extend beyond the pad in the front and will prevent the shorter front edge of the pad from jutting out), and keeping the pad curved as you stitch. The shoulder line of the cover becomes the new shoulder position line.

Keep in mind that the purpose of this type of custom-made pad is principally to bring your shoulder contours closer to near average; it is not to provide the extra height or width called for by any particular style of garment.

The easiest way to use these pads is to attach them to your bra straps with snap tape or to build them into a vestee. (In your case, this also prevents your pads, which are now slightly back heavy, from pulling your clothing to the back.) Then use additional shoulder pads as called for by the garment style; these pads would be attached to the garment itself in the usual way and can be raglan or any other style.

Be aware that you can't always adjust your shoulder contour completely to average using shoulder pads. Fitting alterations to the bodice pattern will often still be needed. In your case, you still need to raise the armscye because your shoulders are square and add width to the back because they are rounded. And you may need to narrow the bodice at the shoulders (you can widen your narrow shoulders by extending the shoulder pads into the sleeve cap up to ¼ in. further than the usual ½ in.).

Uneven shoulders

What alterations are necessary for uneven shoulders? Adding a thicker pad to the lower side only adds to the problem, as it makes the armhole too tight and slightly off grain.

—Dorothy Holman

Dee DuMont replies:

Since almost all garments hang from the shoulders, style alternatives for you are probably limited to selecting less fitted garments such as oversized raglan sleeves and dropped-shouldered styles with deep armholes that will allow room for a larger shoulder pad. If you prefer a more fitted look, there are alteration possibilities.

If the differences from left to right are visually apparent, make a four-quadrant pattern: left front, left back, right front, right back. Let's say that the right side fits and the left side is lower than the right.

On the left back pattern piece, construct an L-shaped slash, vertical from the shoulder seam midpoint (or to one side of the dart) to just below the armscye, then horizontal going all the way through the underarm side seam. Cut this piece apart and slide it down along the vertical line until the shoulder is sufficiently lowered. True the shoulder seam from seam intersection to seam intersection as shown in the drawing at right, and repeat the whole process on the left front, making certain the slash lines originate from the same points on the seamlines as they did on the back pattern piece.

You have now shortened the underarm seam on the left side. This is often all that's needed; you are finished, since the altered seams that will be sewn together are the same length. However, if your body needs the full length of the original side seams, you will want to lengthen them by con-

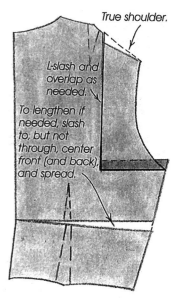

Uneven shoulder

True shoulder.

L-slash and overlap as needed.

To lengthen if needed, slash to, but not through, center front (and back), and spread.

structing a horizontal line perpendicular to center back going from the side seam to—but not through—the center back. Slash the line and spread it open at the side seam an amount equal to the overlap made previously. This returns the side seam to its original length. Be sure to true both center back and the side seam from seam intersection to seam intersection as shown on p. 37, and then repeat the same process on the front.

SHIRTS RIDE TO BACK

Why do some shirt patterns make the garments ride back on the shoulders and pull at the front of the neck? These garments always look sloppy and are uncomfortable to wear. Is there a way to recognize this problem in the pattern, before it's too late?

And enough of these gargantuan shoulder pads already. Some suit patterns ask us to put ½-in. thick pads in the blouse and in the jacket. How do I subtract the allowance for shoulder-pad depth and the added extension of the shoulder line? How much extension is added for different thicknesses of shoulder pads?
—Anna Rich, Elmont, NY

Margaret Komives replies:
One area you can check is the position of the neckline between the front and back patterns. It may be that the neckline is positioned too far toward the back, and as a result, the garment pulls across the front neck.

One quick way to check for this is to measure the difference between the center front and back lengths. I measured four industrial dress forms, sizes 10 to 16, and learned that there was consistently a 2-in. difference between the center-front and center-back lengths (see drawing 1 at left). This tells us that the front pattern should be at least 2 in. shorter than the back. If the difference is less than 2 in., you may need to lengthen the

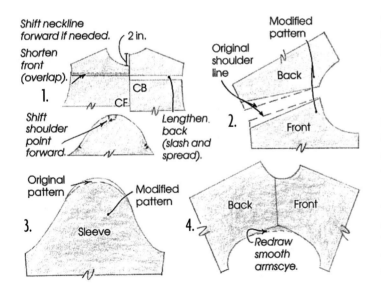

Shift neckline forward if needed.

Shorten front (overlap).

2 in.

CB

CF

1.

Shift shoulder point forward.

Lengthen back (slash and spread).

Modified pattern

Original shoulder line

Back

Front

2.

Original pattern

Modified pattern

3.

Sleeve

Back

Front

4.

Redraw smooth armscye.

back and shorten the front as shown. You also have to shift forward the shoulder mark of the sleeve pattern. I measured several patterns and found the difference ranges from $1\frac{5}{8}$ in. to $2\frac{3}{8}$ in.

As for the shoulder pads, if you plan to wear the blouse and suit together, the pads in the blouse can be removed temporarily. I like to secure pads with snaps, rather than with hook-and-loop tape, because snaps are less bulky.

If you think the height of the pads will be more than you'll like, you can use thinner pads and check the amount of adjustment needed in a fitting. (In my classes, we always play it safe by checking the fit of the garment with the pads in place, because we've found that all too many patterns don't allow enough room for the pads they call for.) If you want to reduce the thickness of the pad by $\frac{1}{4}$ in., then lower the front and back shoulder by $\frac{1}{4}$ in., tapering to the neckline as shown in drawing 2 on the facing page. The sleeve cap must be lowered by the same amount (see drawing 3 on the facing page).

If the shoulder and sleeve are cut too shallow for the recommended pad depth, the garment will pull from the center toward the shoulders. Or the neckline will rest some distance up from the body instead of snugly at the base of the neck. We solve the problem by applying the reverse of the solution above—adding height to the shoulders and sleeve caps.

Joyce Gale adds:

After you've subtracted the height for the pads from the shoulders, be sure to butt the front and back shoulders together along the seamline and redraw the armscye so it's smooth (see drawing 4 on the facing page). If a very thick shoulder pad was called for, the armscye has been straightened quite a bit, and you may have to make it more circular again.

There is no standard shoulder extension in relation to the height of the pad. It varies according to the silhouette desired. A good way to figure out how much the shoulder has been extended is to compare the pattern's shoulder length with a jacket that has no pads and shorten the pattern.

SQUARE SHOULDERS

What causes a collar to droop diagonally and create a pucker running from the second button to the shoulder on my husband's shirts?
—Kazi Pitelka

Correcting for square shoulder

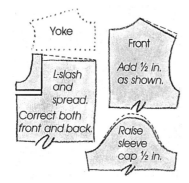

Margaret Komives replies:

The diagonal pucker indicates that the wearer's shoulders are squarer than average. Since men's dress shirts have yokes, this can be fixed by adding to the bodice sections as shown in the drawing at left. To judge how much is needed, I pinch out the excess at the neckline until the pulling disappears. Whatever I've pinched out is the amount I must add at the armscye.

Similarly, a pattern may call for ½-in. shoulder pads, and when they're installed, you get diagonal pulls. To make room for the pads, start stitching on the shoulder seamline at the neckline, decreasing the seam allowance by about ½ in. or more as needed at the armscye. This increases the armscye circumference. Then add the same amount to the top of the sleeve cap (see the drawing at left).

ROUND SHOULDERS, FLAT REAR

I am slightly round-shouldered and absolutely flat in the rear. I cannot get the simplest blazer to fit in the lower back. The jacket back fits across the upper back but is 3 in. too big across the bottom.
—Maxine Raymond, New York

Elaine Rutledge replies:

A rounded shoulder pulls the jacket-back fabric up and away from one's rear. A flat derriére compounds the problem because it needs less roominess, not more.

To fit well and drape nicely, a blazer requires shaping in the upper back, which is accomplished by darts or curved seams. I will assume that the back of your simple blazer is cut on the fold and has no darts, and also that you are not round-shouldered enough to need to add fabric to that area, but only to shape it.

First deal with excess fullness in the hip area. Cut the jacket front and back in muslin, marking lengthwise and crosswise grainlines. Then determine how much excess ease the pattern has relative to your figure, as follows:

Pin the front to the back at the side seams from the waist to the hem. At hem level (or, for a long blazer at your fullest hip level, which you locate on the muslin by measuring down from the base of the neck), measure from center front to center back. From this measurement subtract half the hip measurement given in the body measurement chart of your pattern. The result is half the ease allowance for this blazer, equally divided between blazer front and back.

Then measure your body in the hip area. To establish the side seams on your body, stand sideways to a mirror, with your hand straight down at your side. Bend up your forearm, then raise the elbow straight to the side, keeping the elbow in line with the armpit. Weight one end of a ¼-in. dressmakers' tape and press the other end to the middle of your armpit. Let the tape fall perpendicular to the floor and press it in place on your body. At hip level, mark the position of the tape; this is the location of the side seam. Repeat for your other side.

Measure from side seam to side seam across your front at hip level; do the same for the back. Divide each measurement in half. Subtract these measurements from the pattern's front and back measurements. Compare the results to the ease allowances established earlier. Since your derriere is

Add dart to shape lower back

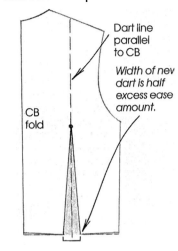

Dart line parallel to CB

Width of new dart is half excess ease amount.

CB fold

flat, you will almost surely have excess width in the back, which you can remove by creating side-back darts.

Fold the back pattern lengthwise, parallel to the center fold line, halfway between the center back and the side seam under the armscye, as shown in the drawing at left. Open the pattern and mark along the fold line from the hem to the upper back below the shoulder blade. This is the center line of the dart; the top of the line is the dart's point. Make the width of the dart at the lower edge the excess ease allowance that you need to remove from the half-back width. You can fine-tune the shaping of the dart during fitting.

Next, try on the fitting muslin. If the crosswise grain between the armholes is not parallel to the floor, but instead curves up in the middle, you'll need to add shaping to the shoulder area by shifting some of the amount of the side-back dart to a shoulder or neck dart. Extend the center line of the dart to shoulder-blade level. This will be the pivot point. Draw a line from this point to the center of the shoulder seam. Cut the pattern on the dart lines to—but not through—the pivot point. Partially close the side-back dart to open the shoulder dart. The shoulder dart line is the inner leg of the dart, not the center of the dart.

Margaret Komives suggests:

A rounded back can be the result of posture, from what I call a "debutante slouch." Both the shoulders and the pelvis come forward, with the result that the lower edge of a jacket hangs away from the body in the rear. This sounds like what you have described.

Make a muslin from your pattern, marking all seams. Pin together the muslin so that at the side seams, the jacket back is about 1 in. higher than the front (see drawing A on the facing page). Try on the jacket. This adjustment should bring the lower edge of the back closer to the body, as well as provide more fabric length over the rounded back. Readjust the back up or down until the drape is satisfactory.

On the pattern, lengthen the center-back seam by the amount that you raised the back at the side seam. Slash the pattern from center back to armscye and center back to side seam at the waist. Spread at center back seam (see drawing B at right). Finally, if necessary, take in the back seams to reduce width across the derriére.

BROAD BACK

I possess a back so broad that it rivals that of many football players, yet my waist and hips are slim. I suffer in anything fitted. As soon as I reach forward my garment grabs across the back, yanking my sleeves up and severely restricting my movements. Adding a gussetlike wedge to the top back seam results in all sorts of ripples and waves near the armholes and lower back, spoiling the beautiful smooth look of a garment such as a tailored jacket. Please help.
—Jacqueline Thibault, Billerica, MA

Joyce Gale replies:

I would add ease by slashing the pattern and spreading it from shoulder to waist. You can do this in three ways, depending on whether your back pattern has a shoulder dart.

If there is no back shoulder dart, slash the pattern from mid-shoulder to—but not through—the mid-waist. Spread ¼ in. to 1¼ in. at the shoulder, tapering to nothing at the waistline (see drawing 1 on p. 44). Then add a shoulder dart about 3 in. to 4 in. long, equal to the amount of spread. The added fabric that has not been sewn into the dart will add the extra width you need across the shoulder blades.

If the pattern has a dart, slash and spread the pattern ½ in. at the shoulder and take up the extra in the dart (see drawing 2 on p. 44).

Adjusting at center-back seam for a flat rear and rounded back

Slash pattern; spread to distribute adjustment amount from fitting muslin.

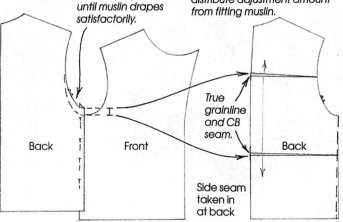

A. FITTING MUSLIN

Shift back up until muslin drapes satisfactorily.

Back   Front

B. PATTERN

Slash pattern; spread to distribute adjustment amount from fitting muslin.

True grainline and CB seam.

Back

Side seam taken in at back

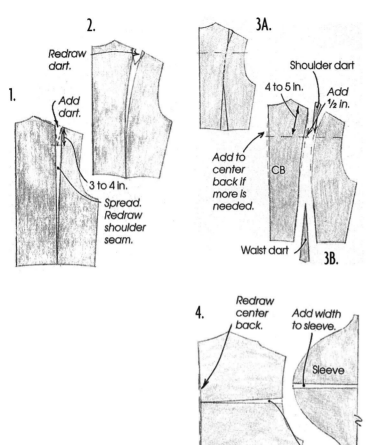

2.

Redraw dart.

1.

Add dart.

3 to 4 in.

Spread. Redraw shoulder seam.

3A.

Shoulder dart

4 to 5 in.

Add ½ in.

Add to center back if more is needed.

CB

Waist dart

3B.

4.

Redraw center back.

Add width to sleeve.

Sleeve

Spread ½ in.

The third method is to create a princess seam and add ease along the new seamline. Cut the pattern on a line drawn from shoulder to waist along the sides of the darts (assuming the pattern has a waist dart) and from dart point to dart point. Gradually add ease, starting with nothing at the shoulder, until you have added up to ½ in. to each piece, 4 in. to 5 in. down from the shoulder; taper back to nothing at the waistline (see drawing 3A at left). Making a seam in the center back and adding slightly through the shoulder blade area, as shown in drawing 3B at right, will also help.

If the armscye is tight, slash the pattern and add ease as shown in drawing 4 below. You have to modify the sleeve, too, so it will fit correctly into the garment.

Britta Callamaras adds:

I would approach correction of a pattern for a broad back and freedom of arm movement as two problems. For maximum freedom of movement, the pattern's armscye should lie about 1 in. below the armpit and close to the line of the natural shoulder joint. Most patterns these days have armscyes much lower and larger than this, which, paradoxically, restricts arm movement; redrawing the shoulder and armscye area of such a pattern takes a lot of fussing.

FORWARD-THRUST SHOULDERS

My shoulders come forward, and I am low-busted and thin down to the bust area. My back shoulder width and breast size fit the pattern size I use, but I have problems with V- and crossover V-necks. How do I adjust the neckline and collar so that the neckline will lie flat?
—Ramona Schall, Midland, TX

Della Steineckert replies:

I suspect that your shoulders come forward because your upper spine is more curved than average. This causes the neck—and collarbone as well—to come forward. It results in hollowness and thinness in the chest area and the lowering of the bust fullness that you mention, and does indeed affect the neckline. You need to lengthen the bodice across center back and shorten it across center front. To make these changes, all you have to shift is the seam allowances, as shown in the drawing below.

Rounded upper back, hollow chest

This figure variation results in too little fabric in upper back, too much in front.

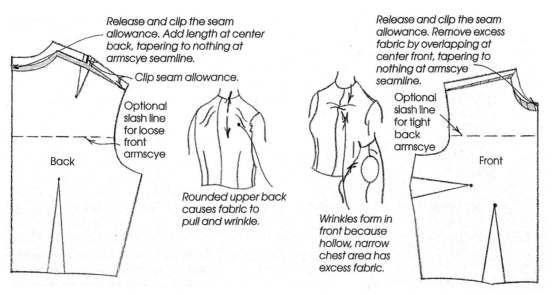

Release and clip the seam allowance. Add length at center back, tapering to nothing at armscye seamline.

Clip seam allowance.

Optional slash line for loose front armscye

Back

Rounded upper back causes fabric to pull and wrinkle.

Wrinkles form in front because hollow, narrow chest area has excess fabric.

Release and clip the seam allowance. Remove excess fabric by overlapping at center front, tapering to nothing at armscye seamline.

Optional slash line for tight back armscye

Front

Removing neckline fullness

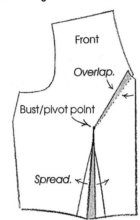

Slash from the neckline and from the waist up to but not through the bust point.

Removing slight excess width

Shifting bodice front sideways at shoulder seam removes some fullness at center.

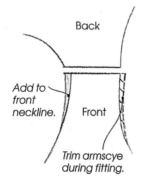

Trim armscye during fitting.

If the armscye is tight in the back and loose in the front after you've made this adjustment, you can also make length changes through the armscye. Slash the back and front bodices horizontally and through the armscye; spread the back and overlap the front uniformly across the bodice. With this adjustment, you'll need to move the shoulder mark at the top of the sleeve toward the front by the amount you spread/overlapped.

With these general length corrections made, adjust the depth of the front neckline if necessary. To raise a V-neckline, lay the pattern over paper, extend the center-front line upward, then redraw the neck seamline to the desired depth, maintaining the character of the original neckline. Reshape collar and facings as well.

Hollowness or thinness of the chest can cause V- and crossover V-necklines to gap because of excess fabric in the neckline. You still need the ease to fit the bust, so to correct the problem, transfer the excess amount to a new or an existing dart in the front bodice, as shown in the drawing above left, or gather the neckline slightly using a tape. This will tighten the neckline against the chest.

A crossover neckline will not fit correctly if the edges rest against the bust fullness. Redesign the neckline so that the edges cross in the cleavage, no higher than the top edge of the bra band underneath the bust.

Margaret Komives adds:

When the shoulders are rounded and curve to the front, there may also be excess fabric in the width of the front bodice. The excess fabric must be removed in order for the front bodice to be smooth. The back bodice may need no alteration.

Try on a muslin and pinch out the excess fabric to determine how much to remove. If it is slight and only in the upper chest, you can add to the neckline at the front shoulder area, as shown in the drawing at left. When you stitch the shoulder seam, this alteration pulls the excess fabric away from the neck and toward the armscye, where you can remove it later during fitting.

For more extreme cases, remove the excess fabric you pinched out at center front by offsetting the pattern center front from the fold of the fabric, as shown in the drawing at right. Or make a similar adjustment to a center-front seam. Make corresponding changes to the facings or collar.

FITTED SLEEVES

The sleeves of dresses, blouses, and especially jackets pull at underarm level when I reach forward, producing horizontal wrinkles at the front of the sleeve.
—Adele Corke, London, ON, Canada

Della Steineckert replies:

Uncomfortable sleeves can have many causes, in addition to the sleeve's being simply too small in circumference for the arm. When the front armscye cuts into the arm joint, it often signals that the bodice back is too narrow. But pulling at the sleeve can also occur if the chest area of the garment is too wide or the armscye isn't wide enough. The garment's armscye must also be long enough to permit maximum joint movement with minimum friction. But if the armscye is too long, the arms can't be lifted easily.

Inadequate bust shaping can also affect sleeve fit because the fabric in the bodice and in the armscye area along with it will be pulled away from the shoulder joint, creating tension in the sleeve. Finally, interrelated factors, such as pattern size, pattern cut, adequate garment ease, and sewing accuracy, can also affect whether sleeves pull at the underarm area.

Removing neckline fullness

To remove a greater degree of excess fabric, offset pattern center front from fold.

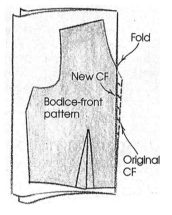

Fold

New CF

Bodice-front pattern

Original CF

Getting to the root of your fitting problem requires analyzing the various factors one by one by comparing some basic body measurements with the corresponding pattern areas. You can then adjust your pattern to correct any discrepancies among the measurements. You'll need a sewing friend to measure the right side of your figure. While being measured, stand erect and look straight ahead. The measurement and ease guidelines presented apply to classic fashion styles with minimum designer ease and average shoulder width, because it's with such styles that good fit is most critical for sleeve comfort.

Check pattern size—First check your pattern size. Measure around your upper torso, high under your arms at chest level. Use this circumference measurement as your full bust measurement when referring to pattern size charts; the corresponding pattern size will be correct for your frame. If your bust cup is larger or smaller than a B (standard for misses' patterns), alter the pattern for bust size (see pp. 74-76).

Measure the body—Next take and record the body measurements pertinent to sleeve and armscye fit, as explained below and shown in the drawing on the facing page. When you record your measurements, include ease allowances. The allowances specified below are for fitted blouses and dresses. For looser styles and for shirts and jackets, add ½ in. ease to all width measurements for the bodice and add 2 in. to the sleeve width.

For *back-shoulder width*, measure from the neckbone at center back over to the shoulder tip (where the outer edge of the shoulder-socket cuff can be felt when you raise and lower your arm).

For *upper and lower arm lengths*, with the arm bent slightly, likewise measure from the neckbone to the shoulder tip, but continue over the shoulder crest, down to the elbow tip, then on to your wristbone. Note the measurements at elbow tip and wrist For your upper arm measurement, subtract your back-shoulder-width measurement from your neck-

Measuring the body for sleeve fit

Stand erect and look straight ahead. Have a sewing friend
take the measurements.

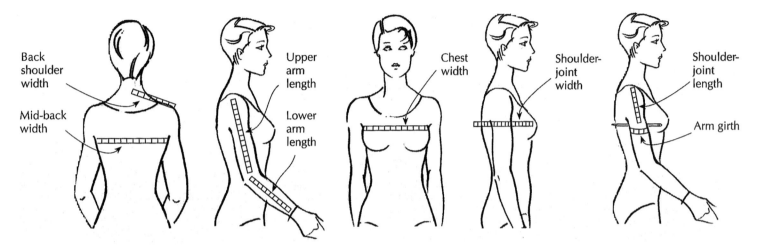

bone-to-elbow-tip measurement. For the lower arm measurement, subtract the neckbone-to-elbow-tip measurement from the total measurement that you noted at the wrist.

Lower and relax your arms. For *mid-back width,* measure across the back
between the creases where the arms meet the torso. Divide the measurement by two and add ½ in. for comfort ease, to allow the back bodice to
move with the arms when they are brought forward. For *chest width,* repeat the measurement procedure on the front above the bust, but do not
add ease.

To measure *shoulder-joint width,* place a thin ruler under the arm and
slide it up to the armpit as high as possible. With both arms lowered,

record the distance between the creases where the arm meets the torso. Divide the number by two (half for the back-shoulder joint, half for the front), and add ½ in. ease to the front measurement only.

To measure *shoulder-joint length*, lower the arms and slide a pencil up against the armpit. Level the pencil by lowering the higher end. Measure from the bottom edge of the pencil up to the crest of the shoulder joint. For a fitted blouse or dress, add ⅝ in. ease to compensate for the underarm seam allowances. For a shirt or jacket, add 1½ in. ease to accommodate a blouse or shirt worn underneath.

For *arm girth*, relax the arms and measure around the biceps area. Add a minimum of 2 in. wearing ease.

Measure the pattern—Press the front, back, and sleeve pattern pieces. Trim multisize patterns along the cutting lines for your size, then draw the stitching lines. Place the patterns over alteration paper on a pinnable surface. For each body measurement, measure the pattern in the appropriate area, marking the pattern where your body measurement falls and also writing down the change (for example, "+½ in.") at each location where it's to be made. The drawing on the facing page shows the measurement areas on a jacket pattern.

First check *shoulder width* (1 on pattern drawing). Using your back-shoulder measurement, measure the pattern from center back straight across toward the shoulder corner (omitting any dart width), and mark where your measurement falls at the armscye area. If you alter shoulder width by more than ¼ in., adjust the sleeve-cap height by the same amount. If you narrow the shoulder, lengthen the sleeve-cap height.

To check *upper-back width* (2), measure from center back at mid-armscye level straight across toward the armscye seamline. Write any change needed at both the mid-armscye level and the base of the armscye; the alteration will taper to nothing at the shoulder and waistline. Using the *chest width* (3) measurement, repeat the process for the front pattern.

Measuring and marking the pattern

Mark each body measurement (including ease) on pattern. Write amount of change needed. Numbers on pattern indicate each location where the same alteration is to be made.

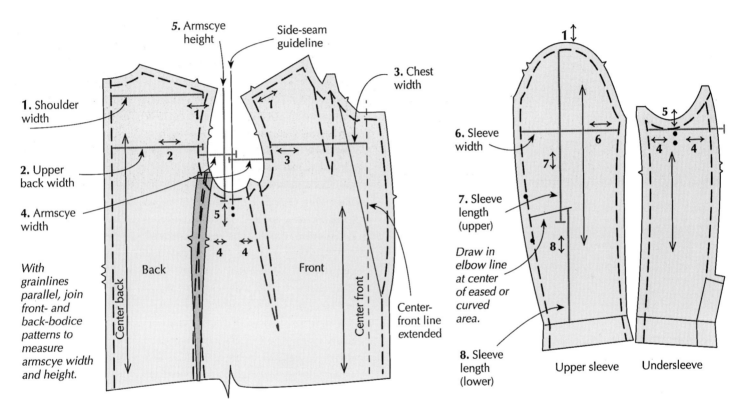

5. Armscye height

Side-seam guideline

3. Chest width

1. Shoulder width

2. Upper back width

4. Armscye width

1

2

3

5

4 **4**

With grainlines parallel, join front- and back-bodice patterns to measure armscye width and height.

Back

Front

Center back

Center front

Center-front line extended

1

6. Sleeve width

7. Sleeve length (upper)

Draw in elbow line at center of eased or curved area.

8. Sleeve length (lower)

6

7

8

5

4 **4**

Upper sleeve

Undersleeve

Check armscye width (4). Match the back- and front-bodice patterns at the armscye/side-seam corners. Extend a guideline from the side-seam position into the armscye space. At mid-armscye level, measure from the back-armscye seamline toward the guideline using your back/shoulder-joint/width measurement. Note any needed width change at the base of the armscye, near the side seam or the underarm mark, and at the underarm area of the sleeve. Repeat for the front bodice and sleeve area using the front/shoulder-joint/width measurement.

Check *armscye height* (5) using the shoulder-joint/length measurement. Measure the back pattern from the level of the shoulder-seamline corner straight down to the stitching line at the base of the armscye. Write any needed change at the base of the armscye and at the sleeve underarm. (When there is a side seam or a sleeve underarm seam, mark both back and front of bodice and sleeve.)

Measure *sleeve width* (6) just below the underarm, using the arm-girth measurement. (For the best way to alter sleeve width, see pp. 58-62.)

To check *sleeve length* (7 and 8), compare your shoulder-crest-to-elbow measurement to the length of the upper sleeve area from the cap seamline to the elbow line. Check the length of the lower sleeve, from wrist line to elbow line, using your elbow-to-wrist measurement.

Make the indicated changes to your pattern using your favorite alteration method.

SLEEVE-LENGTH ADJUSTMENTS

I make wedding clothes and other fancy-occasion costumes, and I have run into a problem: Patterns for long sleeves are generally shaped along the length of the arm, especially at the sleeve hem. How can I know where to place the fitted hemline when I cut out the fabric?
—Mimi Repp, Rochester, NY

Della Steineckert replies:

Measuring the body and comparing it to the pattern is the key. Fitted sleeves have shaping at the elbow, usually in the form of a dart or casing, to allow the elbow to bend. While the finished length of fitted sleeves can vary because of style, personal preference, fashion, and hand shape, the position of the elbow shaping, and thus the sleeve length from shoulder to elbow, must always correspond to body measurement. As you correctly note, any alterations for length must be made before cutting the fabric.

The first step is to determine where on the individual a simple fitted sleeve (one without a shaped hem, a ruffle, and so on) should end. For the average figure, the sleeve should end in line with the wristbone, because this gives the visible hand area a pleasing proportion—about twice as long as it is wide. Sleeves that are too long make the relaxed hand appear pawlike. Sleeves that are too short either look as though they have shrunk or make the arms look long. When the individual is not average in terms of arm length, wrist thickness, or shape and size of hands, the sleeve may look better slightly below or above the wristbone.

When judging length, keep in mind that the sleeve length an individual accepts as "correct" is usually determined by the length she is accustomed to. Thus someone with short arms may accept too-long sleeves as correct, even though the sleeves actually make her arms look even shorter.

After determining where the basic fitted sleeve should end, the next step is to measure the arm. Have your client straighten her right arm at her side (use the right arm because patterns are made for the right side of the body), then lift her hand to form a right angle at her elbow. Place a tape measure from the tip of her shoulder bone down around the elbow tip and on to the wristbone. Record the measurement at the elbow tip (this gives the upper-arm measurement) and at the wristbone. For a sleeve with no shoulder seam, such as a raglan or dolman sleeve, start measuring from the neck vertebra at center back, then to the tip of the shoulder bone, and so on, and measure the same areas on the pattern. In general, if hands and fingers are long and slender, add $\frac{1}{4}$ in. to $\frac{1}{2}$ in. to the total length; if they are broad or short, subtract $\frac{1}{4}$ in.

Now compare the arm measurement to the sleeve pattern. Bring the side seams of the pattern together at the underarm and fold the sleeve in half parallel to the lengthwise grain, as shown in the drawing on the facing page. Then fold the sleeve crosswise in line with the top dart line or through the center of the eased area marked along the back seamline. Unfold the sleeve and mark the center of the wrist line (not where the fold line crosses the wrist line). The drawing shows the marked pattern.

Measure from the seamline at the top of the cap down to the crosswise fold. Compare this measurement to that of the upper-arm length (shoulder to elbow). If the pattern calls for shoulder pads, first add the specified thickness to your upper-arm length (the sleeve and bodice patterns will include added height in the cap and shoulder areas to accommodate the shoulder pad). For puffed sleeves, subtract the amount of puffing from the sleeve measurement.

Measuring sleeve length

Fold sleeve pattern in half lengthwise, parallel to grainline. Fold sleeve crosswise at elbow line. Mark center of wristline.

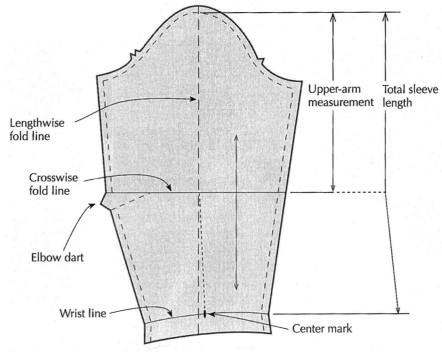

Lengthwise fold line

Crosswise fold line

Elbow dart

Wrist line

Center mark

Upper-arm measurement

Total sleeve length

Adjusting sleeve length

First correct length in upper-arm area of pattern. Then make any further length corrections between elbow and wrist. In this example, length has been added to upper-arm area, and elbow-to-wrist area has been shortened.

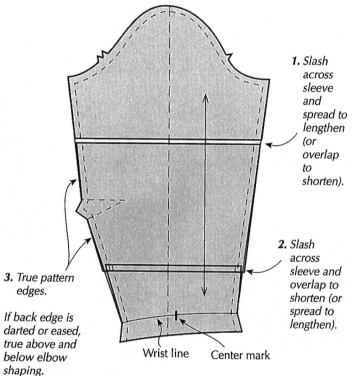

1. Slash across sleeve and spread to lengthen (or overlap to shorten).

2. Slash across sleeve and overlap to shorten (or spread to lengthen).

3. True pattern edges.

If back edge is darted or eased, true above and below elbow shaping.

Wrist line   Center mark

If the upper-arm area of the pattern is too short, slash and spread the pattern as shown in the drawing at left; slash and overlap the pattern if the pattern's upper-arm length is too long.

Next measure the total sleeve length, again starting from the cap seamline to the now corrected elbow line, then to the center mark at the wrist line. Compare the total sleeve measurement to the total arm length. Spread or overlap the lower portion of the sleeve if necessary, making the corrections above the lower edge to preserve the wrist shaping. True the pattern edges from the armscye corners to the elbow line and from there to the wrist line. If the back edge of the pattern has elbow shaping, true from the armscye corners to the top of the dart or eased area, and from the bottom of the dart or eased area to the wrist.

Often, a sleeve is designed so that its lower edge does not fall at the wristbone. When a sleeve has a band with a ruffle at the lower edge, the lower edge of the band should fit as in the basic fitted sleeve, with the ruffle extending below the wristbone. On a chapel-style sleeve, the hem is shaped to a point or an elongated curve and extends partway to the knuckles, partially covering the back of the hand. Across the inside of the wrist, the finished edge of the sleeve lies in line with the wristbone. To measure chapel-style sleeves, draw a wrist guideline on the pattern in a smooth concave curve from side seam to side seam at the lower edge. Use this guideline when comparing sleeve length to arm length.

Long, full sleeves are designed with neither an elbow dart nor ease, but instead have an outwardly curved area along the back wrist edge below the elbow area to permit arm movement. Check the pattern for the length added for blousing. The back edge of the sleeve pattern, near the wrist, should state any amount of blousing; also refer to the fashion illustration. Keep in mind that the amount of length added to the pattern will be twice the amount of blousing (if the pattern states that there is ½ in. of blousing, for example, the sleeve pattern will have 1 in. of additional length). When an elastic casing or drawstring is used to finish full sleeves, measure to the lower edge of the casing. If any of these styles has a band at the wrist, add the finished band width to the sleeve length before comparing sleeve length to arm length.

Sleeves also must have sufficient crosswise ease so that the sleeve encircles the arm smoothly and remains free from tension. Adequate ease at the elbow permits the arm to bend naturally and without stress and the sleeve to return to its normal hanging position. For fitted sleeves made of woven fabric, there should be 2 in. of ease at the elbow. Measure the arm at the biceps line or the armscye line, whichever is larger (see pp. 58-62).

Occasionally, fitted sleeve patterns are not designed with the shaping details needed for arm movement. Unless constructed from a knit, these sleeves will neither permit the elbow to bend easily nor will they allow the sleeve to lower comfortably, and they usually feel and look too short. When this is the case with a pattern, you should incorporate either a dart or ease at the elbow line. First correct the sleeve's total length, then make a mark along the sleeve center to indicate upper-arm length. Slash the sleeve crosswise through this mark, cutting from the back edge to—but not through—the front seamline. Form the dart as shown in the drawing at right. To design an eased area instead, mark the back seamline 2 in. above and below the slashed edges. Before sewing the sleeve, ease-stitch this area.

Adding an elbow dart

If a fitted-sleeve pattern has no elbow shaping, you can add a dart or an eased area. A dart is shown here.

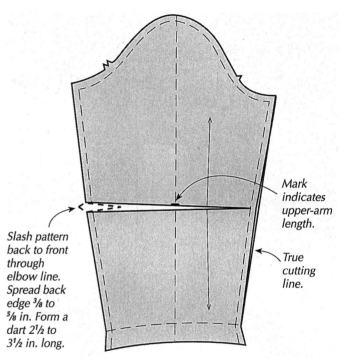

Mark indicates upper-arm length.

True cutting line.

Slash pattern back to front through elbow line. Spread back edge ⅜ to ⅝ in. Form a dart 2½ to 3½ in. long.

LARGE UPPER ARMS

Is there a way to alter set-in sleeve patterns to allow for very large upper arms? I'm tired of the "bat wing" look and would like to use some of the beautiful jacket patterns on the market.
—Sandra M. Cooper, North Aurora, IL

Della Steineckert replies:

There certainly are ways to alter sleeve patterns for large upper arms. Sleeves of incorrect dimension and contour cause problems not only in fit, but also in comfort, appearance, and durability of the armscye area. And sleeve tightness, besides creating a dowdy appearance and the illusion of even larger arms, also causes fitting problems in the surrounding garment areas. A well-fitted sleeve prevents these problems—and is heavenly to wear.

Large upper arms affect sleeves from the cap line (the base of the armscye) to the elbow and require the greatest width increase at the biceps area (about midway between the cap and elbow lines). The extra width should be added evenly across the entire sleeve, but sometimes more is needed in the back half than in the front.

The armscye's dimensions should be left unchanged; you cannot add width at the sleeve's side edges only, as this would change the lower armscye curve and add all the width in one place.

The proper alteration process, shown in the drawing sequence on the facing page, involves pivoting and spreading the pattern at intervals along the cap seamline, thereby distributing the added width across the entire sleeve. You can use this method to add up to 4 in.

First determine how much width you need to add. Lower your arms and have someone measure around the biceps area. To this measurement add 3 in. for a jacket with a typical fitted sleeve or 2 in. for a fitted dress sleeve. Then from this sum subtract the pattern width at the biceps line.

Altering a basic fitted sleeve for large upper arms

This technique adds width but retains the length of the cap seamline. No armscye alteration is necessary.

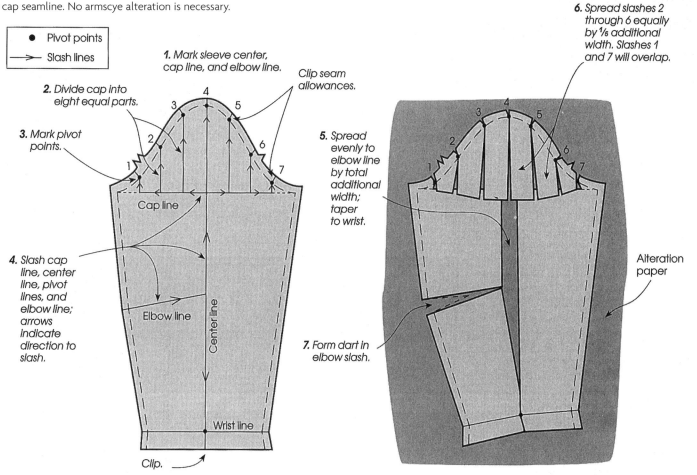

Pivot points

→ **Slash lines**

1. Mark sleeve center, cap line, and elbow line.

Clip seam allowances.

2. Divide cap into eight equal parts.

3. Mark pivot points.

4. Slash cap line, center line, pivot lines, and elbow line; arrows indicate direction to slash.

Cap line

Elbow line

Center line

Wrist line

Clip.

5. Spread evenly to elbow line by total additional width; taper to wrist.

6. Spread slashes 2 through 6 equally by 1/8 additional width. Slashes 1 and 7 will overlap.

Alteration paper

7. Form dart in elbow slash.

Altering a two-piece sleeve for large upper arms

The alteration principles and procedures are the same as for the basic one-piece sleeve shown on p. 59.

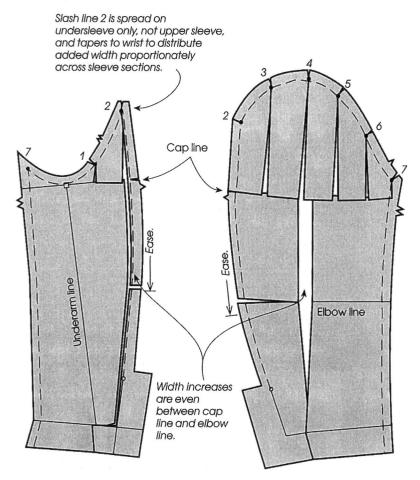

Slash line 2 is spread on undersleeve only, not upper sleeve, and tapers to wrist to distribute added width proportionately across sleeve sections.

Cap line

Ease.

Underarm line

Ease.

Elbow line

Width increases are even between cap line and elbow line.

The result is the total width increase your sleeve needs. Divide the amount by five and write down the result.

Now alter the pattern: First draw the sleeve center, cap line, and elbow line (which is about three-fifths of the distance from the top of the cap to the wrist line) on the pattern. Fold the sleeve cap lengthwise to divide it into eight equal parts. Mark the center of the wrist line. Mark a pivot point where each fold crosses the cap stitching line and the center line crosses the wrist line. (If you are using a multisize pattern, which usually includes only cutting lines, you must first draw the stitching line for your pattern size.) Number the pivot points 1 to 7 from left to right, starting at the pivot point nearest the underarm seam.

Slash the pattern as shown. Clip the seam and hem allowances, leaving $\frac{1}{16}$ in. of paper attached at each pivot point.

Place the pattern on alteration paper. Spread at the slash lines as shown in the drawing. As you can see, the cap height shortens on the altered pattern, but the length of the armscye seamline has not changed.

All sleeve styles can be altered to accommodate large upper arms. Set-in sleeves for fashion jackets fall into three style categories: the standard one-piece sleeve, the modified one-piece, and the two-piece sleeve. The drawing on the facing page shows the alteration for a two-piece jacket sleeve.

To reduce the contrast between the widths of the upper arm and the wrist, and thereby visually slim the upper arm, you may wish to widen the wrist edge by half the upper arm increase.

Margaret Komives adds:

Here's a fast and simple way to increase sleeve width for large upper arms. The maximum amount of width you can add with this method is about 3 in., or slightly more if the sleeve cap is high. To determine how much to spread, measure the circumference of a similarly styled sleeve that's com-

Simple method for increasing width in upper arm

This solution works for increases up to 3 in. in width.

1. *Slash pattern vertically. Spread.*

2. *Take horizontal tuck. Width of tuck is ¼ width increase at cap seamline.*

3. *True cutting lines.*

Needed additional width

New grainline bisects added width.

True.

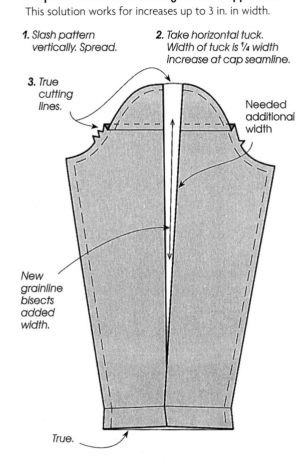

fortable. Measure the same type of garment as you're making (in this case, a jacket), preferably one made of a similar fabric.

Slash the sleeve pattern vertically through the center, from the sleeve cap to the hemline; clip the hem allowance. Spread the pattern to add the needed amount in the upper arm area, as shown in the drawing at left. If necessary, spread a partial amount at the wrist as well. To compensate for the length you've added to the cap seamline, take a tuck across the cap. The width of the tuck should be one-fourth the amount you spread the cap. For example, if you spread the cap by 2 in. at the seamline, the tuck should be ½ in. wide, taking out 1 in. at each side.

When upper arms are large, other body areas are often large also. If you have added width to the bodice at the side seam, lengthening the bodice's armscye seamline, you must likewise widen the sleeve at the underarm seam by the same amount. Then make a corresponding reduction in the amount you spread the sleeve at center.

SLEEVES THAT BIND

I've been sewing my own clothes for 50 years, I've used mega yards of 1-in. gingham, and I am still defeated when I raise my arms in a garment with set-in sleeves. Everything fits fine as long as I stand or sit. But when I drive or eat, the sleeves always bind across the back. Raising the armhole and shoulder does not work.
—*Claire Dolliver, Sarasota, FL*

Margaret Komives replies:
First of all, gingham basics and home drafts are cut with only minimal ease and must be enlarged considerably when converted to garments. Depending on the type of garment, the ease allowed across the back, armscye to armscye 4 in. below the neck, can be 2 in. to 4 in. I've often found, however, that the real problem lies in a sleeve that is cut so narrow that it

simply cannot span the upper arm. Try on your bodice before you cut your sleeve, and measure around your upper arm about 5 in. down from the shoulder point, from bodice seamline to bodice seamline, to see how much sleeve you'll need to go around. (Patterns can vary greatly in this area; a size 12 "fitted" may measure 9¾ in., while one termed "loose fitting" may measure 8½ in.) You need a minimum of 1½ in. ease. Slash the sleeve up the center and spread to correct the width, then take a crosswise tuck to return the armscye to its original size. There's usually plenty of length in the sleeve cap to allow this adjustment, as shown in the drawing above right.

Another option is to round off the back armscye curve of both sleeve and bodice (see drawing below right). Designer Charles Kleibacker pin-fits the underarm: He sits next to the fittee while she extends her arm and rests her hand on his head. The underarm seam of a fitted garment should be 1 in. below the armpit, that of a jacket 1½ in. below. Kleibacker also works with bias bodice and sleeves, which provide stretch to the garment. If you use straight grain, be sure to cut the garment on the lengthwise grain. You'll have the more stretchy crosswise grain going across the sleeve. Also, twills have more give than plain weaves.

A caution: Any change you make in the sleeve must also be made in the armscye. If you slash the sleeve vertically for a heavy arm and simply add to the bodice width at the underarm for fullness, you'll change the curves so that the sleeve ends up twisting when you try to join the seams. If you pivot to gain width in the back, you must do so for the front as well, because pivoting lengthens the underarm seam. But you may not want the extra fullness in front. That's why I prefer to take the compensating tuck in the sleeve as shown.

Sew the underarm seams before inserting the sleeve, whether you are making raglans or set-in sleeves. Doing the cap before the underarm can result in pulling unless the cap is very shallow.

Sometimes we have to compromise a little one way for appearance and a little the other way for comfort.

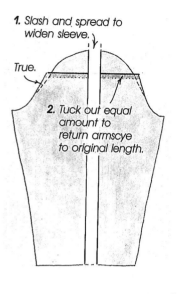

1. Slash and spread to widen sleeve.

True.

2. Tuck out equal amount to return armscye to original length.

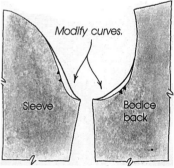

Modify curves.

Sleeve

Bodice back

Chapter 3

the

BUST

FULL BUST

How do I adjust a pattern to accommodate a larger bust size? If I make a size 12 blouse it rips at the bust, but a size 14 gapes at the neck. I also have very wide shoulders.

—Beverly R. Seavey, Madison, WI

Della Steineckert replies:

All misses' commercial patterns, whether a size 6 or a size 14, are designed with a sloper scaled to a B-cup bust. If you are larger or smaller than a B cup, you need to change the bust shaping, not buy a larger or smaller pattern size.

Effect of a large bust on a garment

All commercial patterns assume a size B cup.

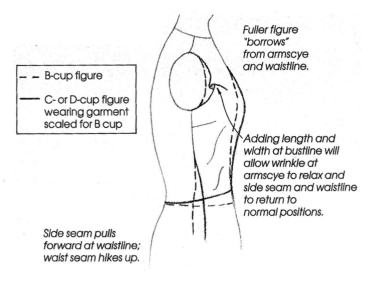

B-cup figure

C- or D-cup figure wearing garment scaled for B cup

Fuller figure "borrows" from armscye and waistline.

Adding length and width at bustline will allow wrinkle at armscye to relax and side seam and waistline to return to normal positions.

Side seam pulls forward at waistline; waist seam hikes up.

Front bodice grade from A cup to DD cup

Bust cup size does not affect bodice pattern in upper chest, shoulder, and neck area; back bodice is identical for all cup sizes.

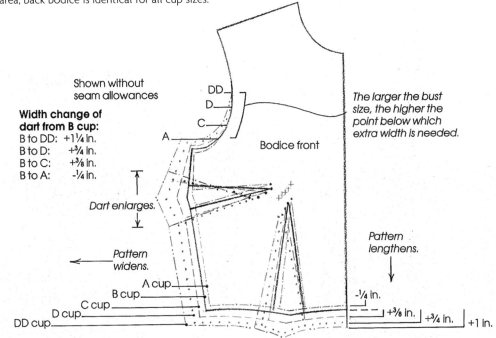

Shown without seam allowances

Width change of dart from B cup:
B to DD: +1¼ in.
B to D: +¾ in.
B to C: +⅜ in.
B to A: -¼ in.

DD
D
C
A

The larger the bust size, the higher the point below which extra width is needed.

Bodice front

Dart enlarges.

Pattern widens.

Pattern lengthens.

A cup
B cup
C cup
D cup
DD cup

-¼ in.   +⅜ in.   +¾ in.   +1 in.

Larger curves need a larger measurement of fabric vertically, horizontally, and diagonally, just as the cover of a soccer ball is larger in every direction than one for a tennis ball. This added length and width forms larger darts at the edges of the bust, where the full-busted figure returns to average. The drawing on p. 65 shows the effect when a woman with a C-cup or larger bust wears a garment designed for a B-cup figure.

Altering for bust size

If your bust size is larger (or smaller) than size B, you'll need to alter your patterns.

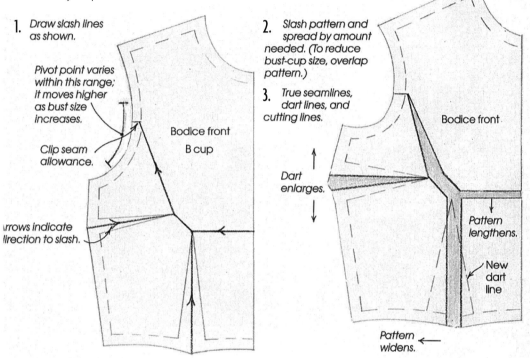

1. Draw slash lines as shown.

Pivot point varies within this range; it moves higher as bust size increases.

Clip seam allowance.

arrows indicate direction to slash.

Bodice front
B cup

2. Slash pattern and spread by amount needed. (To reduce bust-cup size, overlap pattern.)

3. True seamlines, dart lines, and cutting lines.

Bodice front

Dart enlarges.

Pattern lengthens.

New dart line

Pattern widens.

As a woman's bust size increases, not only do the darts get larger, but length increases across the whole front, and width increases from about the middle of the armscye down. Above the chest there is no change. The drawing on p. 66, taken from the McCall's fitting pattern (2718), which, by the way, is a very good fitting pattern, shows a size 6 bodice scaled from an A cup to a DD cup. The back bodice is the same for all bust sizes.

To alter a pattern for a bust size larger or smaller than B cup, make the pattern corrections shown in the drawing on p. 67. Keep in mind that the objective is to increase (or decrease) length and width over the bust area. Even if the bust darts have been pivoted to another location, they will increase (or decrease) in size.

This approach applies also to Laura Treadaway's gaping armhole problem (see p. 79). Her vest requires an alteration for a D cup. The gape at her armhole indicates a need for more fabric over the bust, as explained above. Stitching the gape into a dart will only upholster the fabric to her figure.

If you are full busted, taking your bust measurement at fullest bust level, as you are almost always instructed to do, guides you to an unrealistically large pattern. Breast tissue is all on the front; including it in your torso measurement gives you a pattern that is too big overall (the larger pattern provides more room in the bodice back, where it is not needed). The pattern would still be too tight across the bust because all patterns are scaled to a B-cup bust. To use an extreme illustration, if Dolly Parton were to purchase a sewing pattern based on the usual instructions, she would probably be led to a size 24. However, her torso probably needs a size 10 (I'm guessing). What she should be buying is the size 10, and then altering for her bust.

To prevent the need for extensive fitting in the bodice and to produce a better initial fit, I recommend selecting pattern size by bone structure, not bust measurement, and then altering the pattern for bust size. Measure high around the chest (above the bust) while looking straight ahead with the head raised and the back erect. Inhale naturally and read the tape. You have now measured only the bone structure that forms your rib cage. Use this measurement as your bust measurement when selecting a pattern size. This pattern size in most cases will be in scale to the rest of your torso, although you may need to make minor changes for wider- or narrower-than-average shoulders, and so on. Then alter the pattern for your bust measurement as instructed earlier.

DARTLESS AND PRINCESS STYLES FOR A FULL BUST

Thanks to your "full bust" explanation (see pp. 65-68), I finally know what adjustments to make. But how do I adjust commercial patterns that have no darts or have a princess seam?
—Joyce Arrenson

Della Steineckert responds:

The principle to remember when adjusting for a full bust is that you need to add length and width over the bust area. The width of bust darts (or equivalent shaping) also increases, as the added fabric is taken in at the fabric edge.

The alterations for a dartless bodice and a princess line are shown in the drawings at right. Remember that commercial patterns are designed for a B cup. Spread the pattern by one-half the difference between your own full bust measurement and the bust measurement for your size on the pattern's body measurement chart.

ALTERING PRINCESS STYLES

I sew special-occasion clothes such as wedding dresses for others, and I have particular difficulty with princess seams in front. Women's busts are always higher, lower, or a different size from what the pattern accommodates. Correcting the fit is impossible once the fabric is cut. How should I measure, and how do I translate the measurements to a pattern?
—Mimi Repp, Rochester, NY

Altering for a full bust

A bust larger than a B cup requires that length and width be added to a commercial pattern.

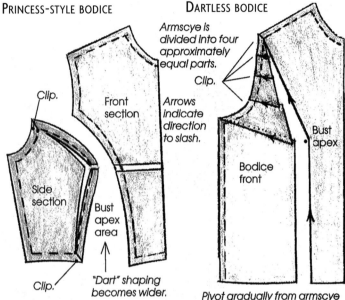

PRINCESS-STYLE BODICE

Clip.

Front section

Side section

Bust apex area

Clip.

"Dart" shaping becomes wider.

Slash pattern. Spread to increase width of side section at apex and lengthen front section. True seamlines and cutting lines.

DARTLESS BODICE

Armscye is divided into four approximately equal parts.

Clip.

Arrows indicate direction to slash.

Bodice front

Bust apex

Pivot gradually from armscye base. To maintain straight lower edge, allow armscye seamline to straighten and armscye base to drop.

Della Steineckert replies:

Princess designs require the most exacting matching of measurements between the figure and the pattern. Although all bodice styles require fitting for both cup size and bustline position, princess-style dresses are almost always fairly fitted, and so proper fitting at the bust is crucial. In addition, the princess seam is a style line that becomes a focal area, and the line must be smooth to be attractive. As you mention, this fitting challenge must be dealt with before you cut the fabric; often both length and width must be added at the bust area, and the usual ⅝-in. seam allowances permit minimal change. Although widening the seam allowances would permit fitting adjustments, you would spend unnecessary time on additional fittings.

Achieving a good fit with a princess style starts with a three-step measuring process that enables you to purchase the correct pattern size for the wearer's frame, determine the bust-cup adjustment, and define the bustline position. The person being measured should wear only the usual underwear needed for the garment style.

If you're measuring yourself, stand in front of a mirror and look straight into it while taking the measurements. Place a ½- to 1-in. wide belt snugly around the waist and adjust it to comfortably define the waistline. (Don't use a string or an elastic because both can sink into the body's soft tissue and may not settle at the true waistline.) The person being measured should inhale normally, holding the breath for each measurement.

First measure the high-bust circumference. Hold the tape high over the shoulder blades in back, under the armpits, and above the bust. Lower the arms, letting the tape expand, and read the tape. Use this measurement as the bust measurement when referring to pattern size charts; this will give you the best pattern size for the individual's frame.

You'll need two measurements to adjust the pattern for bustline position and bust-cup size. First, measure horizontally around the figure at the full bust. Then measure vertically from the center of the right shoulder down over the bust point and straight down to the lower edge of the belt. (The right side is measured because patterns represent the body's right half.) Record the measurements from shoulder to bust point and from shoulder to the lower edge of the belt, adding ¼ in. to the latter measurement for ease.

To determine the adjustments you need to make for bust-cup size (misses' patterns are designed for a B-cup figure), find the difference between the high-bust and the full-bust circumferences. If the full-bust measurement is larger, you'll need to correct the pattern to add width and length over the bust; if the high-bust measurement is larger, you need to reduce length and width. (Someone with an "average" frame and a B cup should find minimal difference or none between the measurements.) To determine the width to be added or subtracted, divide the difference between the measurements by two (because bust tissue is all on the front and the front pattern represents only half the front torso).

Separate the pattern pieces and press the front sections flat. If the pattern is multisized, trim the pattern pieces along the cutting line for the correct size, then draw in stitching lines ⅝ in. inside the cutting lines. Place the prepared pattern pieces over tissue paper.

To alter the pattern, start with the center-front section, which, for princess patterns, is usually altered for length only. Starting from a point on the shoulder seamline directly above the pattern's bust mark, measure down across the bust mark and straight on to the waist level. Note the total measurement. Mark the pattern at the point that corresponds to the individual's bust point (using the shoulder-to-bust-point measurement); label this point "personal bustline." Then find the difference between the pattern's total measurement and the corresponding body measurement.

Correcting bust fit on princess-seam patterns

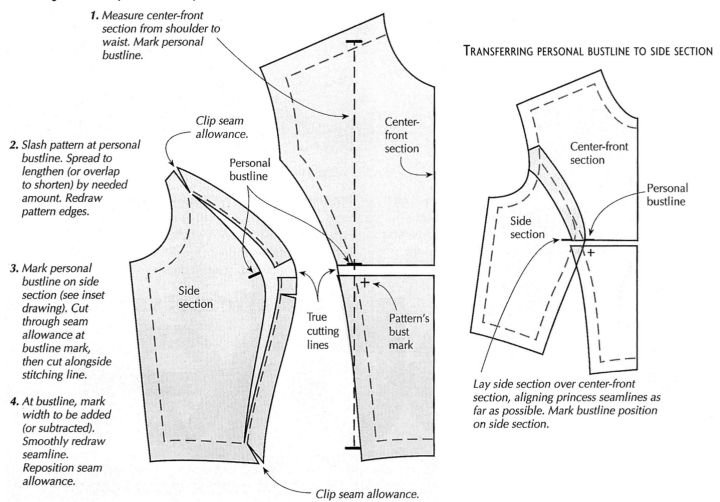

1. *Measure center-front section from shoulder to waist. Mark personal bustline.*

Clip seam allowance.

2. *Slash pattern at personal bustline. Spread to lengthen (or overlap to shorten) by needed amount. Redraw pattern edges.*

Personal bustline

Center-front section

3. *Mark personal bustline on side section (see inset drawing). Cut through seam allowance at bustline mark, then cut alongside stitching line.*

Side section

True cutting lines

Pattern's bust mark

4. *At bustline, mark width to be added (or subtracted). Smoothly redraw seamline. Reposition seam allowance.*

Clip seam allowance.

TRANSFERRING PERSONAL BUSTLINE TO SIDE SECTION

Center-front section

Personal bustline

Side section

Lay side section over center-front section, aligning princess seamlines as far as possible. Mark bustline position on side section.

The difference indicates the length to add if the individual's measurement is longer than the pattern's (or subtract if it's shorter).

Cut across the pattern at the personal bustline mark and spread (or overlap) the pattern by the difference in length, as shown in the drawing at left on the facing page, keeping the center-front line straight. Attach the sections to the tissue paper. Redraw the princess line in a smooth line. The drawing at right shows the alteration when the pattern has a bust dart in addition to the princess seam.

You'll alter the side-front section for width in order to accommodate bustline circumference; this alteration will automatically adjust the length of the princess seam as well. To transfer the personal bustline marking to the side section, lay the side section over the center-front section, matching up the princess seamlines from the armscye (or the shoulder, when the princess seam originates there) as far as possible, keeping the patterns flat, as shown in the drawing at right on the facing page. On the side section, draw a 1-in. mark that is level with the personal bustline mark on the center-front section.

Place the side section back on the alteration paper and tape it to the paper along the side-seam edge. At the bustline mark, cut first through the seam allowance, then cut alongside the seamline, just inside the garment area, up to the armscye (or shoulder) seamline and down to the waist seamline, in both cases stopping just short of those seamlines. Then at the armscye (or shoulder) and the waist seamlines, clip diagonally through the seam allowance corners, leaving the seam allowance attached only at the seamlines. Carefully pivot the seam allowances away from the pattern area. At the personal bustline level, mark the amount of width to be added (or subtracted). Then draw a new seamline from this mark up to the armscye (or shoulder) seamline and down to the waist seamline, giving the new line a similar curve to the old one and making sure the fullest

Altering princess-seam pattern with bust dart

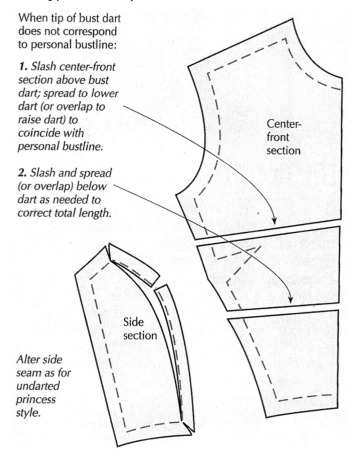

When tip of bust dart does not correspond to personal bustline:

1. Slash center-front section above bust dart; spread to lower dart (or overlap to raise dart) to coincide with personal bustline.

2. Slash and spread (or overlap) below dart as needed to correct total length.

Center-front section

Alter side seam as for undarted princess style.

Side section

part of the curve is level with the personal bustline mark. Reposition the seam allowance with its seamline on the new line, clipping the seam allowance as necessary to allow it to curve to its new shape. Redraw the cutting line in a smooth line.

Measure and compare the length added to (or subtracted from) the princess seam on the side section to that of the center-front section. If the lengths are unequal, raise or lower the lower section of the center-front panel as needed to make them equal. Finally, when cutting the fabric, cut 1-in. seam allowances to permit refining the fit.

SMALL BUST

You've covered fitting and pattern alterations for large-busted women. Now can you provide some hints on altering patterns for those of us who are much less endowed (flat-chested)?
—*Donna Fredericks, Wappingers Falls, NY*

Joyce Gale replies:

Reducing pattern width and length to accommodate a small bust is quite simple. To reduce the space provided for the bust, merely slash the pattern as shown in the drawing at left on the facing page, then overlap the slashed edges. Drawing the slash line to the shoulder, as shown, narrows the pattern slightly through the upper part of the chest. To avoid narrowing the pattern through that area, slash from the bust point to the base of the neckline instead, about an inch away from center front. This alteration works for darted and princess-line patterns. For most dartless patterns fashionable today, it is not necessary to make a correction for a small bust—most dartless patterns look best on small-busted figures.

Altering a pattern for a small bust

Fitting a smaller-than-average bust requires reducing fabric over the bust.

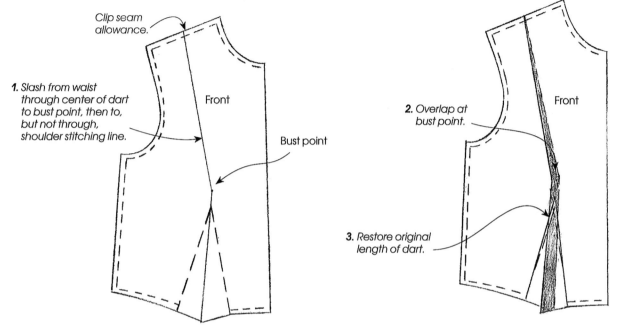

Clip seam allowance.

1. *Slash from waist through center of dart to bust point, then to, but not through, shoulder stitching line.*

Front

Bust point

2. *Overlap at bust point.*

Front

3. *Restore original length of dart.*

To find out how much to overlap, cut the pattern in muslin. Baste the darts and the shoulder and side seams and mark the center-front line. Try on the muslin. Pin the excess fabric at the point of the bust on one side of the body, keeping the center-front line vertical and bearing in mind the amount of ease the style is designed to have. (For ease amounts, check the pattern description to see whether the style is semifitted, loose, and so on, then refer to the ease chart in the pattern catalog.) The amount you have pinned out is the amount to overlap the pattern at the bust point. Redraw the new dart from the waist, as shown in the drawing at right on p. 75, if necessary repositioning it for your figure. Redraw the dart extension.

Margaret Komives suggests:

You can camouflage a flat chest instead of altering a pattern to fit. Altering a pattern to fit a flat chest can emphasize the chest's flatness. If you prefer not to, the easiest alternative is to wear a padded bra or buy the cups sold for swimsuits and insert them in to the bra you wear. By increasing your bust cup size closer to a B (the size commercial patterns are designed for), you can have garments that fit your bust without having to make pattern alterations.

If you prefer not to augment your bust size this way, I would suggest choosing designs that flatter the bustline, such as bodices with yokes and attached fullness in the form of gathers or tucks. When they have enough fullness in the drape, surplice bodices might also be flattering. Before sewing the latter style, try on some ready-made garments to see if you like them.

As for fabric selection, avoid stretch knits and fabrics that drape softly against the body. Choose instead fabrics that hold their own and pool out from the body, as do some polyester crepes.

Dee DuMont agrees:

Selecting a flattering pattern style is the first step. If you don't want to bring attention to a small bust, avoid a tight torso, which will accentuate the smallness of the breast. In general, avoid darted patterns, because darts are designed to throw fullness right over the bust point.

Styles with pleats or gathers that fall from above the bust are good, as are styles that flare from the shoulder. Both throw design ease downward and outward, keeping the focus on the area above the bustline. Cowl necklines, bows, soft ties, and very large collars also draw the eye to them and away from the bust. Lowered armscyes, dolman sleeves, and other cuts that do not feature a tightly fitted armhole are also flattering.

FULL BUST, DARTLESS PATTERNS

Many patterns omit bust darts, and on my figure (large, low bust, but narrow around under the armpits), garments wrinkle diagonally from side seam to bust and don't hang correctly. If I must have darts, what is the best alteration method to use? Better yet, is there a way to correct the pattern without adding darts?
—*Mrs. A. B. Bottini, Novato, CA*

Joyce Gale replies:

There is a current fashion trend that shows many clothes without bust darts. The bust dart is still there, but it has been transferred to other parts of the pattern as extra fullness that hasn't been sewn in, as the drawing at right shows. The larger the bust, the more a bust dart becomes an absolute necessity in all but stretch fabrics if you want the bodice to fit smoothly. Trying to cover a large-busted woman's body without darts would be like trying to cover a large mound of earth that rises in the middle of a flat

Transferring fullness

Slash.

Open.

Bust point

Close.

Slashing and opening to create bust dart

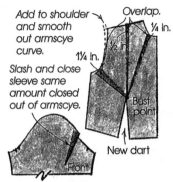

Add to shoulder and smooth out armscye curve.

Slash and close sleeve same amount closed out of armscye.

Overlap. ¼ in.

½ in.

1¼ in.

Bust point

New dart

Front

plain with a piece of fabric without making any pleats or folds in it; it can't be done. I think in your case, it would be far more practical to start with a pattern that already has darts in it. Otherwise, to add darts to a pattern that hasn't any, you must reverse the procedure illustrated above: Slash as shown in the drawing at left; overlap to close the areas that have been opened; transfer all those openings (neck, shoulder, armscye) into an opening for a bust dart. True the seams and adjust the sleeve to match the new armscye length.

Margaret Komives agrees, adding:

The smoothest fit will be obtained with a bustline dart. Before adding a dart, check the length and width of the pattern to be sure you've got enough ease. Measure from midshoulder over the fullest part of the bust to a string tied around the waistline. Compare this to the corresponding pattern length, having allowed some ease for a bit of blouson if it's a blouse or dress, otherwise none. Add length by slashing the pattern horizontally through the bust, spreading the pattern parts, and taping in extra tissue, if needed. The back should be measured similarly. If nothing is needed in front and the bust is large, the back usually needs shortening. Add the same blouson allowance to the back measurement as for the front.

The difference between the alteration made to the front and that made to the back will be the amount needed for the dart. For example, if the front needed 1 in. added and the back needed 1 in. taken up, that would be a 2-in. difference. The dart would be folded 1 in. from a center guideline, taking out 2 in. But before drawing the darts, measure and, if necessary, alter the width of the pattern from side seam to side seam by slashing vertically from midshoulder to waist, then spreading and taping in tissue as described above.

To place the dart: Measure the figure from the shoulder midpoint to the bust point and place a horizontal mark on the pattern accordingly (step 1 in the drawing at right). Measure from center front to bust point and place a vertical mark on the pattern (step 2). Extend the horizontal line to the side seam (step 3). Then draw a guideline from the cross mark to a point on the side seam about 2 in. below the first line (step 4). Draw the dart legs from a point on the guideline 1 in. below the cross point to points half the dart width away from the guideline on the side seam (step 5). Next, tape a strip of tissue about 2 in. wide along the side seam of the front bodice. Fold the dart downward and cut the tissue along the side seam. When opened out, the pattern cutting line will extend correctly (step 6).

If a truly smooth fit is not necessary, the dart can be eliminated: Make a copy of your pattern, adjusted as just explained. Slash through the newly created dart to the cross mark. Also slash through the area of a waistline dart and almost to the cross mark. Close the bust dart, and the waistline dart will open to compensate. If this dart isn't stitched, it's called a released dart. This design would result in considerable fullness at the waist to be gathered or tucked.

Placing a dart

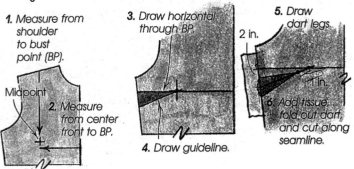

1. Measure from shoulder to bust point (BP).

Midpoint

2. Measure from center front to BP.

3. Draw horizontal through BP.

2 in.

4. Draw guideline.

5. Draw dart legs.

2 in.

1 in.

6. Add tissue, fold out dart, and cut along seamline.

VEST GAPES AT ARMSCYE

No matter what style vest I sew there is always an unsightly gape in the front armhole between the bust and shoulders. I have a size 16 (D-cup) bust and size 8 shoulders that are somewhat square. I have tried lowering the shoulder seamline on the front to no avail.

Also, when we are told to measure from the shoulder, over the apex of the bust and down to the waist, should the tape measure be next to the skin between bust and waist or held in a straight line?

—Laura Treadaway, Marshall, AR

Measuring distance over bust for patterns with straight or curved darts

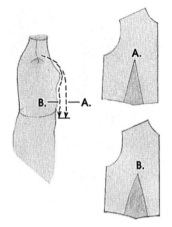

Joyce Gale replies:

First, the measuring question. Hold the tape in a straight line from the bust point to the waist for straight darts (line A in the drawing at left), but next to the skin for curved darts or close-fitting princess lines (line B). Since you are large-busted, you should add a little extra length to the bodice, or the bodice will pull up from the waistline.

Gaping in the armhole of a vest occurs because part of the ease of a basic dart has been pivoted into the armscye (and is unstitched) to achieve a more flat-busted look. This excess fullness causes the gape, which will seem to radiate from the bust point This is why lowering the shoulder seam would not solve the problem.

The best solution would be to close the dart by putting in a princess seamline. To find out how large the dart needs to be, which determines the curve of the seamline, make a quick sample. Cut the vest pattern in muslin and baste it together, running a line of stitching along the edge of the armscye to prevent stretching. Pinch and pin the gape closed and mark on the muslin what you've pinned out. Rip out the stitching and lay the muslin flat.

On the pattern, connect the two darts with a curved line as shown in the drawing at left on the facing page. Mark a cross line at the end of each dart. These are reference marks for aligning the two front sections after you have cut them apart.

Trace two pattern pieces, following the legs of the darts as shown. You may have to add length to the edge at the armscye to make the seams the same length. Add seam allowances to the two seamlines, extending the cross marks into the seam allowances.

Adding a princess seamline to a vest to eliminate a gaping armscye

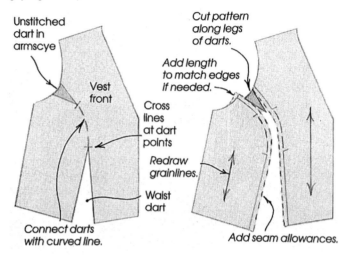

Unstitched dart in armscye

Vest front

Connect darts with curved line.

Cut pattern along legs of darts.

Add length to match edges if needed.

Cross lines at dart points

Redraw grainlines.

Waist dart

Add seam allowances.

Eliminate armscye gap in princess-line vest

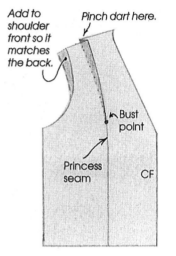

Add to shoulder front so it matches the back.

Pinch dart here.

Bust point

Princess seam

CF

Margaret Komives adds:

If the vest pattern already has a standard princess line, you can alter it by taking in the princess seamline at the shoulder, as shown in the drawing at right above. Stitch a muslin. Then pinch the fabric at the shoulder, tapering to the bust until the gaping goes away. Redraw the seamline to fall along the sides of the dart. Add the same amount to the shoulder seam at the armscye so that front and back shoulder seams will match. (You can make this correction in the actual garment by adding to the shoulder before cutting the fabric.)

If your pattern doesn't have a princess seam and you don't care for that style, you can make a shoulder dart instead. Pinch out a dart in the shoul-

Eliminating armscye gap in darted vest

Pinch out a dart in the shoulder.

Extend shoulder to match back.

Bust point

Or, pinch out a dart in side seam, extending armscye by equal amount.

---

der and extend the shoulder width as described previously (see drawing at left). Or pinch out a dart in the side seam, first lengthening the seam into the armscye by the width of the dart.

Although many women prefer not to have darts, some kind of shaping is a necessity for those with a full bust, unless the fabric is stretchy. Darts can be camouflaged in fabrics with texture or a fine print.

NARROW BACK, FULL BUST

My back and shoulders are too narrow for a size 8, but my bust is too big. I've been told to buy a larger pattern and take in everything but the bust, but this is more trouble than enlarging the bust. If the pattern has darts, I can enlarge them, but what about tailored jackets? I've only succeeded on jackets with a seam running through the bust all the way to the shoulder (not a princess line), but that limits my choices.
—Julia Royster, Raleigh, NC

Dee DuMont replies:

From a visual standpoint, you may want to build out the shoulder just a bit and use a shoulder pad to assist in the fitting. This can create a pleasing, triangular silhouette that diminishes an excessively busty appearance and is especially effective in jackets.

Generally, when your bustline is full in relation to your frame, purchase a smaller pattern and alter for the bust only. The neck, shoulders, and back will probably have a more pleasing fit than would have resulted if you had selected a larger size.

To do an accurate bust alteration: Locate your bust point, where you'll need added fullness. Work on the dominant (larger) side of your body and take the following four measurements from the visual center of the bust: to the shoulder intersection with a jewel neckline; the center front on a jewel neckline; the opposite bust; and the center front at the waistline. Transfer as many of these measurements as possible to the bodice pattern, drawing lines or arcs as needed. Normally the first and third measurements are the easiest to locate. The lines cross near your bust point. Or approximate the measurement by holding the pattern up to your body, aligning center front and the neckline, and mark the center of the bust area.

A simple bust alteration that can be spread (or overlapped) is a modified T-cut. Beginning at the waistline hem of the blouse front pattern piece, draw a line parallel with the center front (or grainline) going directly to the bust point. Continue the line from the bust point up to the shoulder area, going to—but not through—the shoulder seam. Draw a lateral line from the bust point to—but not through—the side seam, perpendicular to the first line. Cut and spread the pattern as required for each side (the pattern piece is actually only half the front).

What happens next depends on the cut of the garment. For an unfitted blouse or jacket, continue the added fullness to the hemline by positioning the side pattern section parallel to the center front section, as shown in the drawing at right above. For a more fitted waist, swing the side section in at the hem, as shown in the drawing at right below, maintaining the increase at the fullest part of the bust.

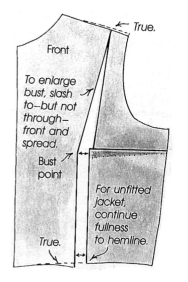

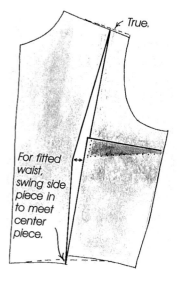

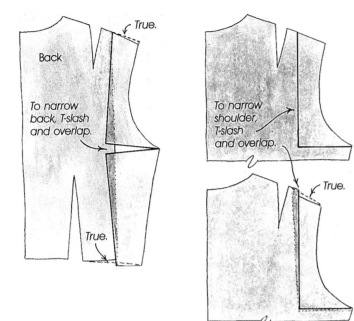

To narrow the back, prepare a modified T-slash as discussed previously, but this time the lateral slash will go to—but not through—the intersection of the side seam and the armscye line. Instead of spreading, overlap the pattern as shown in the drawing at top left.

To reduce the shoulder length, construct an L-shaped line beginning in the center of the shoulder line on the back (or to one side of the dart if there is one) and going down the back parallel with the grain (or center back). Construct a perpendicular line to—but not through—the armscye seam about halfway between the shoulder and the underarm as shown in the drawing at top right. Cut from the top down, and overlap the piece at the shoulder seam the amount it needs to be reduced. Then true the shoulder line. The front shoulder seam will require a similar alteration to ensure that front and back seams are of equal length.

JACKET HEM RIDES UP

What is it about a jacket's cut that causes the hemline to ride up and stand away from the body in center front, back, or both on cropped styles? I've tried easing in fullness over the bust at the side seam (cutting the front longer). I've even tried cutting a curved hemline. With both I've had mixed success.
—Kazi Pitelka

Margaret Komives replies:
I've found that adding to the length by slashing and spreading the pattern through the bust area for the amount determined by a muslin test garment and darting to take up the slack at the side seams so the front matches the back (see the drawing at left on the facing page) work in most cases. This sounds like what you did; perhaps you didn't add enough. For a full bust,

we also add width at the underarm side seam. With this adjustment, the garment can be fitted to the body and any excess trimmed away.

If your bust is very full, major corrections in the form of the grand slash up (actually three slashes as shown in the drawing at right below) may be the answer. Add to the center-front length as shown, then take up the added length in the side seam with a bust dart. By lowering the grand slash origination point at the armscye, you can create less fullness in the front shoulder area above the bust, while allowing the necessary fullness in the bust area. The grand slash is major surgery, so make a test garment, pin-fitting initially on the original seamlines to be sure your additions won't distort the garment's cut.

Correcting a hem that rides up in front

The grand slash

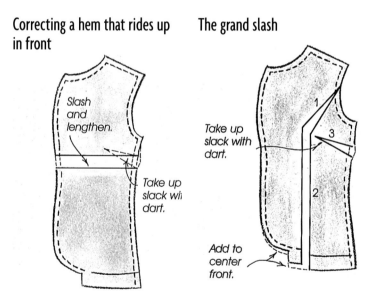

Correcting hem flare in back

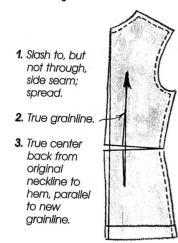

1. Slash to, but not through, side seam; spread.

2. True grainline.

3. True center back from original neckline to hem, parallel to new grainline.

As for the back, when I first saw that little flared extension at the tail of a jacket, I put on my thinking cap. If a jacket has a vent that spreads, we correct it by taking a horizontal dartlike tuck at the waistline center back tapering to nothing at the side seam. So why not now do the opposite? We cut a jacket except for the back, which we cut out of test fabric and slashed as shown in the drawing at left. The jacket fit beautifully! We also had to decide what to do with the grainline. We trued the center-back seam as shown. A different design might dictate otherwise. The same problem could be caused by a rounded back. In this case, slash at mid-back instead of at the waist. For a cropped jacket, you might prefer to cut the upper part on grain since there would be very little of the jacket below the slash.

FULL BUST, HOLLOW UPPER CHEST

My problem is fitting sleeveless garments around the bust. I have a C-cup bra and a hollow upper chest. I've been able to alter patterns to account for this, except on sleeveless garments. They always seem to gape around the armhole, at the bust.
—Jane Harrington, Bala Cynwyd, PA

Dee DuMont replies:
There are several solutions, and they involve a shift from mere pattern alteration into pattern making.

One possibility is to fold out the extra as a bust dart in the armhole area to reduce the circumference of the armscye while allowing for the fullness of the breast. Be sure to adjust the armhole facing to correspond. If you don't want an actual dart in that area, the dart can be converted to fullness elsewhere in the bodice and be controlled there as a dart or pleats (see the drawing at left on facing page). A princess-line seam that comes from the armscye area is another possible solution, for the two sides of such a seam actually create a darting effect; this style would be relatively easy to adjust (see the drawing below right).

Another fitting problem that often accompanies this body type is gaping in a scooped neckline. A more covering bodice actually hangs from the shoulder and neck, draping to the bust area. If the neckline falls in the hollow area above the bust, gaping can occur. This, too, can be corrected with an overlap in the pattern tissue. Pivot through the bust point and transfer the resulting fullness to a dart or into the waistline area, as the drawing at right below indicates. If it still gapes, the neckline can be further tightened by redrawing the shoulder seam where it meets the neckline, once again creating a very slight "dart."

When all the adjustments have been made, be sure to alter the collar or facings to reflect the changes in the bodice.

Overlap to avoid gaping armhole

Adjusting for gaping neckline

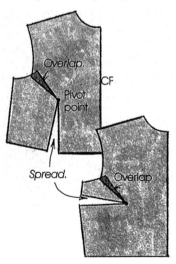

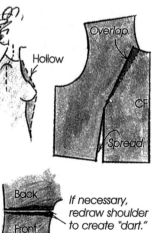

Chapter 4

❖

FROM THE WAIST DOWN

SKIRT WAIST ADJUSTMENTS

How can I prevent a skirt from riding up and forming a fold just below the waistband? Because I have a short waist, I cut the waist edge of the pattern along the stitching line instead of the original cutting line. And I still must fold the pattern ¼ in. just above the hip area to lower the waistline further.
—Mary Duhame, Weston, ON, Canada

Della Steineckert responds:

A horizontal fold such as you describe is usually the result of a garment area below it that's too tight on the body. The too-tight area prevents the skirt fabric from hanging down as it normally would. A skirt's circumference is smallest at the waist, becoming gradually larger to the hem. If the skirt is too tight at the hip, it will ride up on the body until a lower, larger section reaches the hip area. Since the upper edge of the skirt can't rise above the waistband, the fabric is forced into a fold just below the band.

You mention having a short waist (a shorter-than-average upper torso). You should correct for this at the bodice, not the skirt waistline. If you also have a short lower torso, this may be contributing to your problem.

Lowering the waistline of the skirt, which you are doing, will accommodate a short lower torso. However, your method simultaneously narrows the darts and makes the waistline slightly larger, effects that may or may not be desirable. In any case, the fact that the fold persists despite your alterations definitely indicates a need for more width below the fold, that is, through the hips.

Keep in mind that at the waist, high hipline, full hipline, and buttocks' and abdomen's crests, a skirt made of woven fabric should be at least 2 in. larger in circumference than your body measurements. Its waistband must be at least 1 in. larger than your waist measurement. This extra width permits normal body movements, draping of the fabric, and the tucking in of the tail of a lightweight blouse. To maintain the ratio of the necessary wearing ease and the pattern's design ease when altering the pattern, adjust it only by the difference between your own body measurements and the standard body measurements from the chart on the pattern envelope or guide sheet.

To determine the necessary adjustments, first measure your waist and full hip (the area where your hips look broadest) with the measuring tape snug but not tight and level around the body. Also measure your hip depth—the distance from the bottom of the tape at your waist to the bottom of the tape at your full hip—on your right side.

Write down each measurement and next to it the standard body measurement. Then subtract the smaller from the larger measurement and note the difference, or alteration, required.

Alter the pattern, starting with the waistband. Measure the length of the pattern from closure point to closure point (excluding any overlapping edges). Add 1 in. to your waist measurement (more if you prefer a looser band), and compare the sum to the waistband measurement. Divide any difference by four (you'll alter the waistband equally in each of its four sections), and note the adjustment needed on each section and on the front and back skirt pieces at the waistline near the side seamline. Alter the waistband pattern as shown in the drawing on the facing page. Next divide by four the alteration amount for your full hip and note this

Altering a skirt to add width at sides

If skirt rides up and forms a fold below the waistband, it may be too tight through the hips.

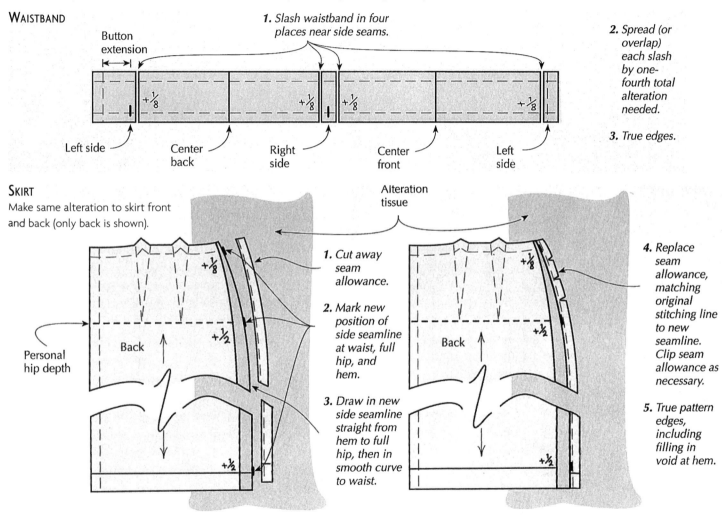

WAISTBAND

Button extension

1. Slash waistband in four places near side seams.

$+\frac{1}{8}$ $+\frac{1}{8}$ $+\frac{1}{8}$ $+\frac{1}{8}$

2. Spread (or overlap) each slash by one-fourth total alteration needed.

3. True edges.

Left side — Center back — Right side — Center front — Left side

SKIRT

Make same alteration to skirt front and back (only back is shown).

Alteration tissue

Personal hip depth

Back

$+\frac{1}{8}$

$+\frac{1}{2}$

$+\frac{1}{2}$

Back

$+\frac{1}{8}$

$+\frac{1}{2}$

$+\frac{1}{2}$

1. Cut away seam allowance.

2. Mark new position of side seamline at waist, full hip, and hem.

3. Draw in new side seamline straight from hem to full hip, then in smooth curve to waist.

4. Replace seam allowance, matching original stitching line to new seamline. Clip seam allowance as necessary.

5. True pattern edges, including filling in void at hem.

amount near the side seamline on the front and back pattern pieces at your hip-depth level (measure from the pattern's waist stitching line down along the side seam) and at the hemline, too.

To alter the front and back pattern pieces, separate the side-seam allowances from the actual garment areas by carefully cutting alongside the seamline, just within the garment area, as shown. (With a multisize pattern, first trim the pattern on the cutting line for your size and draw in the stitching lines.) Place tissue under the trimmed pattern edge and anchor the pattern area to it, leaving the seam allowance free. Make the alterations to the pattern as shown in bottom drawing on p. 91.

When a pattern is altered for a hip contour that is more curved than average, additional length must be added at the waist (a larger curve needs more length as well as width) to restore the smooth curve of the waist edge. Lay the front and back patterns side by side, matching the side stitching lines near the waistline, as shown in the drawing on the facing page. Redraw the waist stitching line so it forms a smooth curve across the seamline and rejoins the original waist stitching line one-third to one-half the distance to center front and back.

When you first make up a skirt with these pattern alterations, include 1-in. seam allowances at the side and waist edges. Baste the skirt and ease it onto your prepared waistband, aligning the side and center markings of the band and the skirt. Take in or let out the sides and waistline as necessary to smooth the fabric and perfect the hip contour but retain the ease. Then correct the pattern accordingly. In the future, cut the skirt with the usual ⅝-in. seam allowances and don't baste.

Refining a waist edge

When the skirt has been altered to make the hip curve more rounded, the waist edge requires refining. (Shown without seam allowances.)

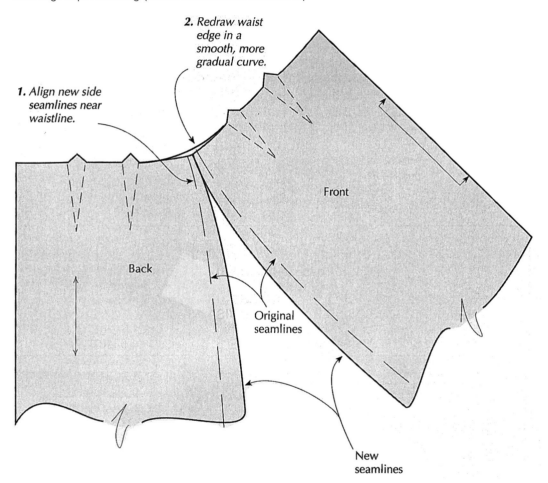

2. *Redraw waist edge in a smooth, more gradual curve.*

1. *Align new side seamlines near waistline.*

Front

Back

Original seamlines

New seamlines

Margaret Komives adds:

If you need to remove length from the waist edge of skirts, it's probably because you're short from the waist to the full hip. To determine your hip depth, tie a string around your waist and measure along your side from the string to where your hip is fullest. If the distance is less than 8 in. (standard hip depth), you do, indeed, need to remove length at the skirt's upper hip area. Cutting on the skirt's waist stitching line will help, but it makes the waistline seam longer. A better way to correct your pattern is to slash the front and back pattern pieces horizontally about 4 in. below the waistline and overlap the patterns by the needed amount, as shown in the drawing on the facing page.

In addition, repositioning the waistband relative to your body and to the skirt will help. As a rule, patterns are designed so that the figure's waistline is at the stitching line of the waistband's lower edge. However, when the band is placed around the waist, its lower edge always sits slightly below the waistline. The degree to which it settles depends on the figure's contours and the waistband's width. When the upper hip area is fuller than the area above it, the band will rest slightly higher. When the above-the-waist area is fuller, the band will rest slightly lower. The wider the band, the lower it will rest.

Altering a skirt for short lower torso

When waist-to-full-hip depth is less than 8 in., the skirt needs to be shortened through hip area.

1. Slash pattern horizontally about 4 in. below waist.

2. Overlap slashed edges by personal hip depth subtracted from 8 in.

3. Redraw dart stitching lines.

True pattern edges.

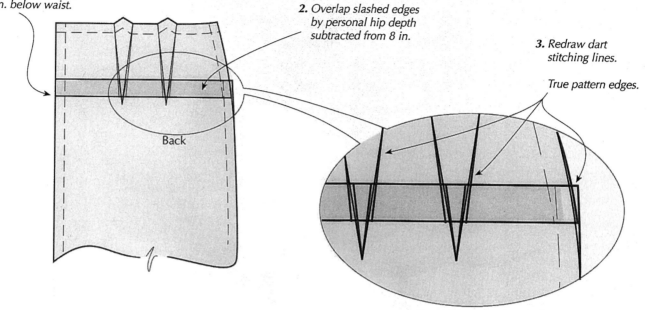

Back

In any case, when the band is attached to the skirt and the skirt is worn, the band will settle below the wearer's waistline and the skirt likewise will want to settle lower. If the skirt is fitted through the hips, the waistband will be unable to settle, and a horizontal ripple such as you describe will form below the waistband.

To solve this problem, first fit the skirt with the cut edge of the waist, rather than the stitching line, at the body's waistline. When you have fit the skirt as well as possible, pin a length of firm waistband interfacing (such as Armoflexxx Plus or Ban-rol) or the actual interfaced waistband, folded to the finished size around your waist.

Then chalk-mark around the base of the band to mark the stitching line for attaching the band. If you've used the actual waistband for marking, also mark the position of the side seams on it—a big help in distributing ease when you attach the waistband to the skirt. This alteration is also helpful for those who have a high hip, full tummy, or swayback.

Once you've determined the stitching line for a basic pattern, you cannot simply use that stitching line position for a waistband of another width. Because the band's width affects how low the band will sit on the figure, you must fit a different-width waistband separately.

FITTING PANTS

My waist is 25½ in. and my hips 33½ in. I have a flat stomach, flat derrière, and hollow hips. Add well-developed thighs and calves from bicycling. I need to know how to adapt women's pant patterns to fit my proportions.
—*Gloria Horsey, Waynesboro, PA*

I have a swayback and high tummy, which make skirts, pants, and some dresses take on an oddly slanted waistline, but a level waistband always looks bad. How do I fit this problem?
—*Sue Hodgson, St. Louis, MO*

Britta Callamaras replies:

Whenever there are multiple fitting problems, it's best to check the pattern by fitting a muslin. Try the following procedures.

Start with a pattern that accommodates your widest back hip measurement, widest tummy measurement, and the most developed thigh area. Cut the pattern with generous seam allowances from fabric similar to the weight of what you plan to use for your real project.

Make a fitting band that fits your waist snugly, but comfortably, to hold the pants muslin in place as you make adjustments. Stitch a 1-in.-wide band from firm fabric, and add hooks on one end and small safety pins for eyes on the other.

With chalk, mark crease lines that follow the grain on the pants front and back. Machine-baste the inseams and the crotch seam, leaving a zipper-length opening in front. Overlap the seamlines at the front opening and pin it closed so it lies flat. Leave the side seams unstitched.

Try on the fitting band and hook it at center front. Put on the pants, right side out (see drawing A on p. 98). Tuck the front securely under the fitting band and adjust the pants until the lengthwise grainlines (crease lines) hang straight and the crosswise grain is level at the hips. There may be gathers at the waist, but don't worry about them for now. Then arrange the back the same way. If the pants won't hang properly under the buttocks, you'll have to correct this first. Remove the pants and add or subtract length (see the pants-measuring schematic in the drawing on p. 99), and change the crotch shape and/or inseam extensions. Put the pants back on and check that the inseams hang straight down the legs and halfway between the front and back. Smooth the back and front, working toward the sides, with one hand on the back hip and the other on the front, both 5 in. to 7 in. below the waist. Pin the side seam with wrong

Fine-tuning pants fitting

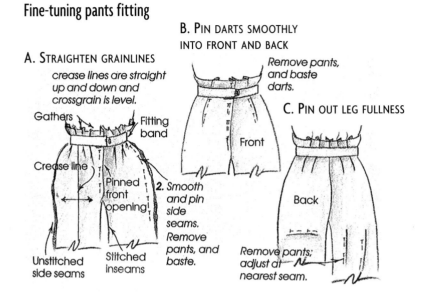

A. STRAIGHTEN GRAINLINES

crease lines are straight up and down and crossgrain is level.

Gathers

Fitting band

Crease line

Pinned front opening

Unstitched side seams

Stitched inseams

B. PIN DARTS SMOOTHLY INTO FRONT AND BACK

Remove pants, and baste darts.

Front

2. *Smooth and pin side seams. Remove pants, and baste.*

C. PIN OUT LEG FULLNESS

Back

Remove pants; adjust at nearest seam.

sides together, first toward the waist, then down to at least the thigh/hip line, or as far as you can reach without bending, making sure that the side seams are at right angles to the floor. They should fall halfway between front and back at the sides, even though the seam allowances will probably be uneven at the top or side. When seen from the front or back, seams may curve in at the waistline, but the crease lines should not be distorted.

Remove the pants, mark the seams with chalk, and indicate with a safety pin the position of the raw edges in relation to each other at the top. Baste the side seams. Establish new crease lines in each leg by matching inseam to side seams and pressing. Put on the pants. Arrange the waistline fullness into darts or into the seams (see drawing B above). Pin on the right side of the garment since that's the easiest way to get an accurate shape of the body underneath. (This procedure is for size and fit. You can arrange the fullness into released pleats or tucks later.) Make sure darts point to the fullest parts of the body, ending 1 in. to 1½ in. above them, and that the fabric lies smoothly, even though the darts may not be in the usual places. Mark the waistline seam at the bottom edge of the fitting band and remove the pants.

Mark the placement of the pins on the wrong side. Machine-baste the darts and try on the pants before cutting and sewing in fashion fabric. If the legs seem large, just reach down below the crotch and pin out the excess as needed, in front or back or both (see drawing C on the facing page). Make corrections at the nearest seam. This may shorten the crotch or narrow the front or the back, or do all three.

Margaret Komives adds general pants-fitting advice:

When part of the figure extends, there is a need for additional fabric in both length and width. Fabric must be added where it's needed. That is why it's so much more effective to fit a muslin for alterations rather than simply measuring. Measurements tell us how much is there; they don't tell us where it is. In fitting pants, there are three dimensions to be considered (see the drawing at right): lower torso length from waist to crotch, depth of body, and circumference around the figure at the widest part—be it at hips, tummy, or derrière—noting where side seams are located. (For an in-depth look at pants fitting, see pp. 66-71 in *Fit and Fabric from Threads*, The Taunton Press, 1991.)

First find the lower torso length. An easy way to do this is to subtract the inseam from the side seam measurement of a pair of pants that fit. Measure the front pattern at the side seam from waistline seam to a horizontal line that runs through the intersection of the inseam and crotch seam. Adjust front and back equally on the lengthen/shorten pattern line accordingly.

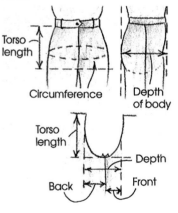

CRITICAL FITTING DIMENSIONS FOR PANTS

Torso length

Circumference

Depth of body

Torso length

Back

Depth

Front

IDENTICAL WAIST-TO-WAIST MEASUREMENTS

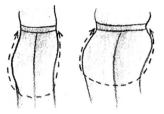

Vastly different torso lengths, depths, and circumferences may yield identical waist-to-waist measurements.

OPTIONS FOR FITTING HIGH TUMMY

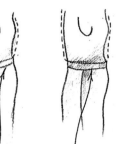

Added length covers, but emphasizes, tummy.

Keep waistband level. Blouse covers high tummy.

Then find the depth by measuring from front waist to back waist through the legs, and compare this to the pattern. Any difference in the depth is adjusted at the inseams. I usually measure the front and back of an existing pair of pants for depth because ease is already included. Adjust each pattern piece as needed.

You can't just add to the torso length when the waist-to-waist measurement is longer than the pattern's. A very tall, thin person may have the same waist-to-waist measurement as a short, stout person (see the drawing at left). Adding length, when what you may really need is depth, will cause smile-shaped wrinkles along the center-front seam. *Note:* Center front should always be cut on grain, and center back should often be cut as close as possible to the grain for a better drape.

Last of all, check the circumference measurement. To increase, slash and spread each pattern vertically from waistline to hem, as needed.

You can add to the front torso length when the tummy rides high, with the results as shown in the left-hand drawing at right. Instead, I encourage people to reestablish the pants waistline parallel to the floor (the waistband rides low) and let the blouse, not the pants, cover the tummy, as in the right-hand drawing at right. By the way, a level waistband is more comfortable when sitting.

PANTS FOR A PEAR-SHAPED BODY

I'm rather rounded, full in the hips, with heavy thighs. My greatest problem is making pants fit in the back seat and upper legs. I've narrowed the problem down to the cut of the crotch and the angle of the center-back seam.
—Joyce Gossett, Hayti, MO

Margaret Komives replies:

You're right on target with your statement that the problem lies largely in the cut of the crotch and the angle of the center-back seam. I prefer to do the length correction first, then add width at the inseam, as I'll explain later. These corrections are easy to modify at the fitting stage if necessary.

A very angular center-back seam has the effect of one huge dart in the middle of your pants. At the base of a dart there will be fullness. In the case of pants, that fullness will end up right where you want it least if you are making dress pants that you want to hang nicely from the waist. If you prefer snug thighs, as with jeans, you'd need more of an angle.

The crotch curve shape is often a problem because a woman's pelvic structure differs from that of a man's, and while now and then you find a pattern that is cut accordingly, most are not. In most cases the back crotch curve should be lowered and the center-back seam straightened, as shown in the drawing at right. This correction is best accomplished after the inseams are sewn together.

Here is a good way to go about fitting pants: First determine the length of the lower torso from waist to crotch by subtracting the inseam length from the side-seam length of an existing pair of pants that fit in that area.

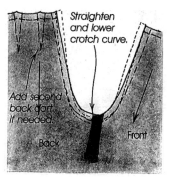

Straighten and lower crotch curve.

Add second back dart if needed.

Back

Front

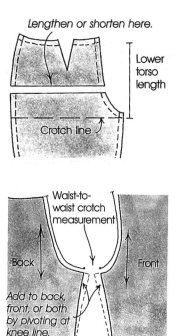

Lengthen or shorten here.

Lower torso length

Crotch line

Waist-to-waist crotch measurement

Back

Front

Add to back, front, or both by pivoting at knee line.

If the front pattern does not have a crotch line, it's easy to draw one. It should be perpendicular to the grainline and end at the point where the center seam meets the inseam (see the drawing at top left). Compare this measurement to that of the front pattern, and alter on the lengthen-or-shorten line if need be. The back pattern would be altered by the same amount. (No ease is needed because the existing garment already has it and because this seam can be lowered but never raised.)

Next, measure the waist-to-waist (crotch) seams of the existing pants, front and back separately. Measure the pattern by standing the tape measure on its side, and compare these measurements. If the pants' measurement is greater than that of the pattern because the figure is deep from front to back, add to the inseam as shown in the drawing below left. The addition should be made here rather than at the top of the pattern because the pattern has already been corrected for length.

The same correction may be needed for heavy thighs such as you describe. First of all, choose a pattern that has front fullness. This will serve a dual purpose. It will not only tend to disguise the problem, but it will also provide more of the fullness needed.

It doesn't work to measure the thigh and then try to measure the pattern pieces because there is comparatively more fullness in the back area just under the seat. The extra is usually needed in the front, but if the back fullness is not adequate there can still be pulling in the front.

As an added precaution, add to the inseams, especially the front, as shown in the drawing below left. This fullness can be removed easily in fitting if it is not needed. More may also be needed at the front side seams, or the creases might be thrown off center.

Next, check the hip measurement, including the high-hip area. Often a figure will be larger about 3 in. down from the waist than it is at the actual hipline (about 8 in. down). Measure both areas, but not snug under the tummy. Then check the pattern.

There should be about 3 in. of wearing ease at the full hip by today's standards. Tucks need more. Take a minute to analyze the figure from the side. Will more be needed in the front because of a large tummy, or in the back because of a large derrière? If so, measure the front and back separately from side seam to side seam. The needed amount can be added at the side seams or by slashing the pattern vertically and spreading. The needed amount may differ in the front and back.

As for the high-hip measurement, it can often be accommodated by not stitching the tucks down for a full tummy or by shortening, narrowing, and curving the darts for a full backside. Sometimes an additional amount at the side seam is needed, but not often. Every figure is different.

PANTS FOR A FLAT SEAT

I am a professional dressmaker, but I still can't get a pair of pants to fit me properly. I have a flat seat and am thin and without a lot of curves. The front of pants looks great and the side seams are straight, but there is always too much fabric below the seat in the back.
—Carol A. White, San Bruno, CA

Joyce Gale replies:

Adjustments to pants should be made by a second person, who can see the pants on you and can rip and fit while you're wearing them.

I assume that you're working with a slacks style (one that hangs straight down from the buttocks), as opposed to jeans. Excess fabric below the seat is caused mainly by a back-crotch measurement that is too long for your measurements and a back-crotch curve that is too deep. These two causes work hand in hand—the deeper the crotch curve, the longer the crotch length—but they must be corrected separately.

Construct the pants in muslin or, better yet, an inexpensive fabric similar to the fabric that you'll be using. Have your helper pin a dart horizontally across your upper hip, taking in as much as is necessary at the center back, and tapering to nothing at the side seam, to make the pants hang straight down from the point where your buttocks curve out the most. Fold this amount out of the pattern, as shown in step 1 of the drawing on the facing page, thereby shortening the back-crotch length.

You may still have excess width across the seat, a result of too deep a crotch curve for your particular body shape. Have your helper pin out the fullness in the pants with a long vertical dart. Mark the dart on the pattern. Then transfer the dart to the crotch and inner leg seams so that the amount of fabric removed from these seams corresponds approximately to the amount pinned in the dart, as shown in step 2 in the drawing on the facing page. (Note that you can make this adjustment to purchased slacks as well.) Do not lower the crotch in the area indicated or the front and back inseams will not match. The adjustment already made to the back inseam may cause it to be slightly shorter than the front inseam. If so, stretch the back between knee and crotch when you sew. Cut out the revised pattern in fabric, try on the pants again, and make any further adjustments.

Once you're achieved the right fit in one fabric, you'll need to compensate for different-weight fabrics or stretchier fabrics. And your pattern adjustments will be different for each basic pants style (tight jeans, slacks, or baggy pants).

Adjusting pants for a flat seat

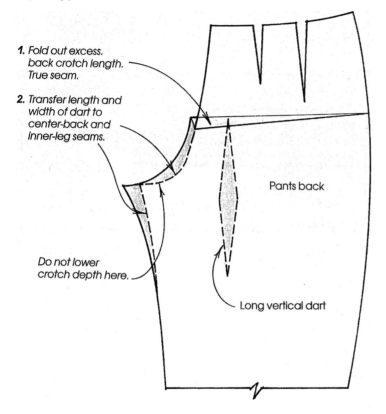

1. *Fold out excess. back crotch length. True seam.*

2. *Transfer length and width of dart to center-back and inner-leg seams.*

Do not lower crotch depth here.

Pants back

Long vertical dart

Margaret Komives suggests:

First remove the fullness created by the angled center-back seam and the darts. Cut the center-back seam more on grain (as shown in step 1 of the drawing below). Make the darts smaller, and if there are four darts, per-

Another way to adjust for a flat seat

1. A sloped center back acts as a dart; adjust CB so it's on grain.

2. The deeper the darts, the more slope the fanny area has; decrease shaping by making darts smaller.

3. Crotch is too deep; move crotch curve inward at inseam.

4. Take in CB on grain. Redraw crotch curve to meet CB.

5. Take in side seam as needed.

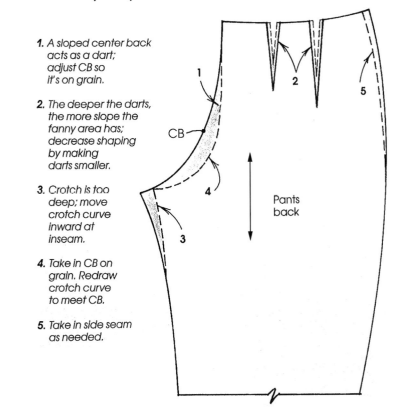

haps change them to two (step 2). A long, sweeping inseam also creates fullness, so take the elongated point off the inseam (step 3).

If the crotch curve is shallow (the pants have horizontal wrinkles under the seat), lower the crotch curve (step 4)—fullness cannot be removed from the back if the crotch curve is too high. Then see if you can take in the center-back seam at the waistline. Finally, take in the back at the side seams (step 5). Every one of these alterations, including taking in the side seam, can be done without changing the pants front.

Pants creep up

Since I went from a size 9 to 16 with pregnancy, the front legs of shorts and culottes tend to ride up into the crotch as I walk (and I've noticed other large-size women with the same problem). I'm not hippy, nor do I have heavy thighs. The shorts and culottes are a loose style, not tight anywhere. What alteration can I make to ready-to-wear and to sewing patterns to correct this?
—Sher Lee, Rapid City, SD

Margaret Komives replies:

For walking (as well as sitting) comfortably, it is important to have enough fabric in the back inseam to allow for freedom of movement, especially in fabrics that have little ease. As the leg moves forward, if there is not enough room in the back inseam for a good stride, the fabric pulls at the front, causing the pant legs to ride up.

As a result of weight gain, probably in the tummy area, your body depth (roughly the distance from your front to your back as you stand in profile) increased. The increase in body depth calls for added fabric at the inseam, as you can see from the drawing below. Although your pants may feel loose (and they may well be loose in other areas), they probably don't have adequate fabric at the inseam for comfort during walking.

The back or the front inseams, or both, may need to have fabric added. In your case I'd try the back first (heavy thighs would indicate a need to add to the front inseam).

To alter a pattern, slash from the back- (or front-) crotch seam to—but not through—the inseam, as shown. Spread the pattern to lengthen the crotch seam and add width at the inseam simultaneously. If purchased

Adding to inseam to accommodate increased body depth

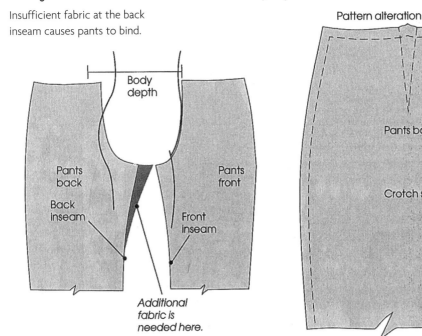

Insufficient fabric at the back inseam causes pants to bind.

Body depth

Pants back

Pants front

Back inseam

Front inseam

Additional fabric is needed here.

Pattern alteration

Slash from crotch seam to inseam. Spread. True cutting lines.

Pants back

Crotch seam

Inseam

pants have any extra width in the seam allowance of the inseam, you could restitch the inseams to gain a little more room.

Another possible cause of your problem may be a shallow back-crotch curve. Redraw the back-crotch seam with a deeper curve, as shown in the drawing below. You can even make this correction with purchased shorts. Turn the shorts inside out and fit one leg inside the other. Restitch the curve deeper, and then trim the seam allowance.

Deepening a back-crotch curve

A deeper, more rounded back-crotch curve makes pants more comfortable.

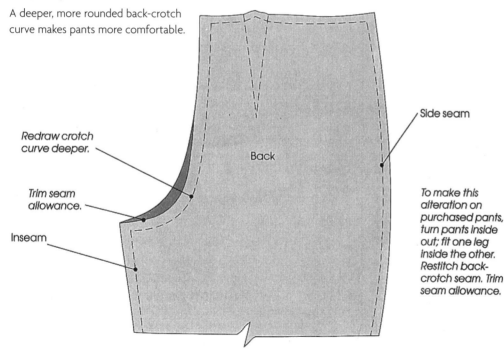

Redraw crotch curve deeper.

Trim seam allowance.

Inseam

Back

Side seam

To make this alteration on purchased pants, turn pants inside out; fit one leg inside the other. Restitch back-crotch seam. Trim seam allowance.

Shortening crotch length

When crotch is too long, pants can be uncomfortable for walking.

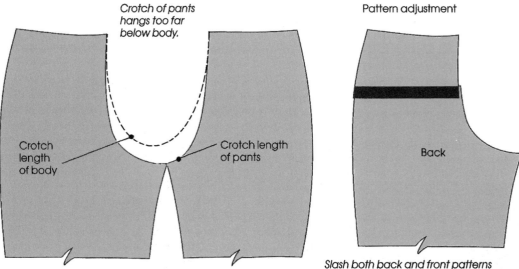

Crotch of pants hangs too far below body.

Crotch length of body

Crotch length of pants

Pattern adjustment

Back

Slash both back and front patterns horizontally. Overlap. True cutting lines.

Dee DuMont agrees, and adds:

Surprisingly, another situation that can cause pant legs to ride up into the crotch is when the crotch length of the pants is too long, and the crotch hangs down 3 in. to 4 in. below your body, as shown in the drawing above. This could be caused by the style of the pants or by your own body shape. In this case, the moving leg hits against the crotch seam, making it tug uncomfortably in the rear, and the seam moves up and out of the way to make more room for the striding leg.

Since you mention a size change related to pregnancy, I presume you are buying the larger size in order to get the waistband size you need. But if your frame continues to be closer to a size 9, you may not need the crotch length provided in a size 16.

On purchased pants, try pinning out some of the excess length near the waistband, taking a horizontal tuck across the back or the front or both. If this solves the problem, remove the waistband and shorten the pants from the top by the amount you pinned out. You may have to cut off the top of the zipper.

To check the crotch length of a pattern, first measure the back- and front-crotch seamlines, standing a tape measure on its side and not including the seam allowances at waist and inseam. Add the front and back measurements together. Then measure your own crotch length (bring a tape measure from your waist at the back, through your legs, and to your waist at the front), and compare the two. In order to be comfortable for walking, the crotch length of pants should be 1 in. to 2 in. longer than your crotch length.

If you need to shorten the crotch length on a pattern, make a horizontal slash across both the back and front pattern pieces, as shown in the drawing on the facing page. Overlap the back and front patterns each by half the excess length.

If the crotch length is okay, the riding up may be caused by lack of ease in the thigh area, particularly in the front. If, as the leg moves forward during walking, it doesn't find quite enough room in the front of the pant

Adding to pleat to increase fullness

Adding fullness in pants front eases pressure on garment leg during walking.

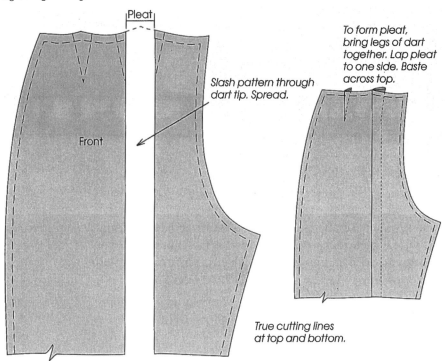

Pleat

Slash pattern through dart tip. Spread.

Front

To form pleat, bring legs of dart together. Lap pleat to one side. Baste across top.

True cutting lines at top and bottom.

leg, the pressure on the pant leg will push the fabric upward. If this is the case, the solution is to add extra fabric to the front of the pattern by slashing the length of the pattern vertically and spreading it at the waist, as shown in the drawing above. You can control the added fullness by stitching a pleat at the waistline, as shown in the drawing. (It isn't possible to make this correction on purchased pants.)

PANT LEGS TURN IN

The legs of my pants turn to the inside of the ankle. Any tips for preventing this?
—Mrs. A. H. Bottini, Novato, CA

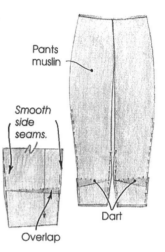

Pants muslin

Smooth side seams.

Overlap

Dart

Joyce Gale replies:

I would suggest cutting the pattern in muslin to try out the following alteration: Sew the crotch seams, darts or pleats, side seams, and inseams down to the point where the legs start turning in. Then, starting at the side seam, pin a dart across each leg, in the back and (if needed) front, as shown in the drawing at top right. Pinch in no more than 1 in. until the legs hang straight. Continue pinning the rest of the leg seams together. You may need to add additional fabric to the inseam to make the edges meet. Mark the seams and new hem with a pencil.

Now rip the pants apart, put the muslin back on your pattern, and transfer the corrections. Where a dart is pinned on the muslin, you should slash and overlap the pattern and tape the pieces together, so that the pant leg is one continuous pattern piece. Redraw the side seam and the grainline.

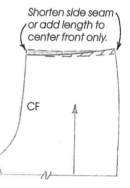

Shorten side seam or add length to center front only.

CF

Margaret Komives adds:

Sometimes a round tummy pulls pants upward in the center front, causing the legs to appear to twist to the inside. You can add length to the center front or shorten the side seams of the back and front at the waist (see the drawing below right). Both methods will have the same results.

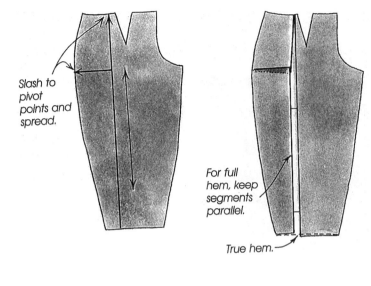

Slash to pivot points and spread.

For full hem, keep segments parallel.

True hem.

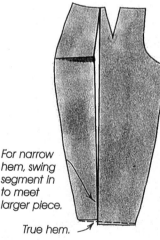

For narrow hem, swing segment in to meet larger piece.

True hem.

HEAVY THIGHS

I have heavy thighs and I find that most slacks hug my legs in a way I do not like, so I have stopped wearing them. Is there another way?
—*Shirley Mendlowitz, Lake Worth, FL*

Dee DuMont replies:

Full thighs can be visually diminished by careful pattern selection. Pants that have deep pleats at the waist can look good, as can harem styles and long culottes. However, two very basic alterations can make even the most tailored cut look good on your body.

The standard alteration to increase the area at the hip and thigh is a modified T-slash. On the pants-pattern front and back (you'll probably want to distribute this additional ease on both pattern pieces), draw a line parallel with the grain, running from the hem to—but not through—the waist seam. Then at the fullest point of the hip, construct a perpendicular line that runs to—but not through—the side seam, as shown in the drawing at top left. Starting at the hem, cut the pattern to the pivot points and spread the long pieces apart to increase fullness.

From the fullest point down you have two choices, depending on the pant style. You can continue the increased amount (¾ in. for example) all the way to the hem by placing the outer pattern segment parallel to your original cut, as shown in the drawing at top right. Or, if you want the narrower look at the hem, swing the pattern segment in until it touches the inner segment, as shown in the drawing at bottom. In either case, the pattern will overlap at the lateral slash to remain flat, and the hemline will require truing to return the pattern to its original character.

This alteration can also be done on skirt patterns.

MATERNITY CLOTHES

Can you offer some advice on altering patterns for maternity wear?
—Jane Harrington

Margaret Komives replies:

Unless the weight gain is such that it affects the arms and shoulders—it usually isn't—you can use your existing patterns by making some simple changes. Blouses that have yokes are great. The only change needed is slashing the bodice front vertically and spreading it a few inches. Then either gather or tuck it onto the yoke front, and the rest of the blouse can stay as is.

My favorite maternity jumper was made from a loose-fitting jumper pattern. I left extra at the side seams; this I formed into a deep inverted pleat. Tabs just above the waist held it closed. The last few months, I removed the tabs to release the pleats.

Many dress patterns can be converted to maternity wear by creating a yoke in the front bodice. Simply slash the pattern where you'd like the yoke to end. Be sure it's well above the bustline. Then add a seam allowance to each slashed edge and slash the bodice section vertically to add fullness in the width.

You could also slash the pattern vertically in several places from the shoulder down to the hemline and then spread the sections at the hemline to create a flared effect.

Adding a maternity panel

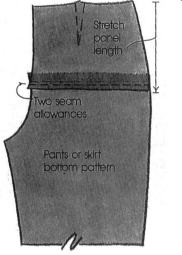

Stretch panel length

Two seam allowances

Pants or skirt bottom pattern

Multiple slashes for large increases

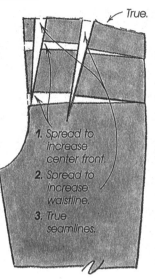

True.

1. Spread to increase center front.
2. Spread to increase waistline.
3. True seamlines.

For pants or skirts, simply insert a stretch panel (available at fabric stores) at the top front from side seam to side seam. Cut away the pattern the length of the panel minus 1¼ in., which you'll need for two ⅝-in. seam allowances, as shown in the drawing at left.

Dee DuMont adds:

In general, alterations for maternity wear are similar to other pattern adjustments. For the abdominal region, of course, pattern spreads are well in excess of the recommended ½ in. per slash; for pants or a skirt, both the center front and the waistline must be increased unless a stretchable maternity panel is planned for the garment. To achieve a smooth extension to the front waistline seam and to the center-front seam between the waist and the crotch, I would do two or three smaller slashes and spreads on each seam (see right-hand drawing at left), rather than the typical single slash of an average pattern-fitting adjustment. True from low point to low point on each slashed segment to create a smooth curve as shown.

Often during pregnancy, the body changes in areas other than the abdomen, and it is wise to monitor increases in the bust measurement (including near the arms in the back), additions in the high-hip area within 3 in. of the waistline, and additional all-over weight gain that may well necessitate a larger pattern size than has been purchased in the past.

Uneven hips and legs

For a figure with one leg and hip longer than the other, how do you blend the two sides at seams?
—Priscilla Wyman

Dee DuMont replies:

It depends on the extent of the difference. Most of us differ from left to right, with the dominant (i.e., right-handed or left-handed) side usually slightly more developed. With age, these differences can become more noticeable and can require special fitting attention, although the general wisdom says to avoid over-fitting so as not to draw attention to minor differences. Changes in the fashions selected can even eliminate the need for alterations. Select garments that hang from the shoulders and have no waistline seams, such as jumpers, dropped-waist dresses, and unrestricted jumpsuits. Garments with elasticized waistline seams also work well, often requiring little more than rehanging the hem.

When you do want a close fit, alterations are in order. For minor differences, I suggest cutting the larger side a bit wider at the hip, higher at the side seam along the waistline, and longer, while cutting the smaller side as usual. The excess seam allowance area will allow you to pin-fit the larger side right on the body.

For a significant and visually apparent difference between the two sides of the body, you'll need a four-sided pattern, i.e. right front, left front, right back, left back. To increase the (left) hip height, draw a line perpendicular to the grain, going from the side seam in the hip area to—but not through—the center-front line. Spread the pattern apart at the side seam to increase the length, filling in with tissue paper (see the drawing at right). Do the same on the back (left) pattern piece, beginning at an adjacent point along the side seam.

Pants for uneven hip and leg

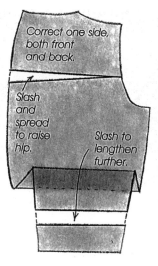

Correct one side, both front and back.

Slash and spread to raise hip.

Slash to lengthen further.

Skirt for uneven hip and leg

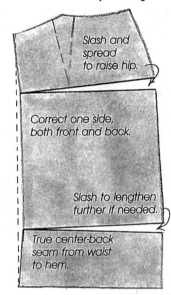

Slash and spread to raise hip.

Correct one side, both front and back.

Slash to lengthen further if needed.

True center-back seam from waist to hem.

To further lengthen the left leg in pants, construct a lateral line perpendicular to the grain either above or below the knee; slash and increase the pattern the desired amount, spreading evenly across the pattern piece, as shown. Do this on both the left front and left back pieces, again ensuring that the slash lines originate at the same point on both the outside and inside seams.

When you are working with a skirt, four pattern pieces are required, but all the slashes on the left side will go to—but not through—the center-back or center-front seam so that their length, which will eventually be joined to the unaltered right side, will be unchanged. After the side seam increases are made, be certain to true the center-back and center-front seams to return them to their original character (see the drawing at left). If the pattern calls for placing the center front on the fold, merely open up the fabric and butt the right and left side patterns to each other, cutting one layer. Be careful to note the correct side of the fabric when cutting this piece.

FLUCTUATING WAISTLINES

What can I do to make my fluctuating waistline size more comfortable?
—Andi Weiss Bartezak

Britta Callamaras replies:

If you make skirts or pants with a center opening, front or back, you can add a gusset at each side seam for an adjustable waistline. This can be almost invisible if hooks with thread eyes are used for the closure. Sewn with a tailor's buttonhole stitch, these closures stay on forever.

To make the gusset on a front-opening garment, cut the waistband so you have two front halves plus seam allowances, and a back plus seam allowances.

Sew the skirt side seams to within 3 in. to 4 in. of the waist, ending above the high hip or tummy line. Press the seams open, including the seam allowances of the opening. Press the waistbands in half lengthwise. Cut a rectangle of garment fabric using a selvage edge as the width to prevent stretch. Make it 4 in. wide, and an inch longer than the opening plus the pressed width of the band. Fold and press the selvage under an amount equal to the pressed width of the band. Sew the bands to the skirt, right sides together, along the waistline seam.

Mark the gusset's center and side seam at the top, on the fold, ¾ in. to 1 in. from the center line, as shown in the drawing at right. Pin the gusset to the skirt, right sides together, matching the just-made mark with the band's seamline at the fold and the gusset center line with the side-seam opening point. Sew the gusset/skirt side seam up to the fold in the band. Trim the gusset to match the skirt seam allowance. Turn the band to the inside and stitch the band end along the gusset seamline (see the inset at right). Clip the seam allowance as shown, and turn. Finish the band with a stitch-in-the-ditch.

Sew two hooks at top and bottom of front waistbands. Sew matching eyes at the end of the back bands, and two more pairs of eyes on each gusset. You now have an adjustable placket on each side of the waistline that will grow up to 4 in. to accommodate weight change, hormone fluctuation, and Thanksgiving dinners.

Gusset for fluctuating waistline

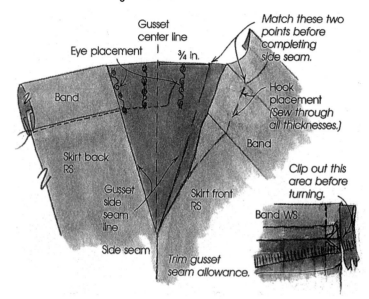

Gusset center line

Eye placement   ¾ in.

Match these two points before completing side seam.

Band

Hook placement (Sew through all thicknesses.)

Band

Skirt back RS

Clip out this area before turning.

Gusset side seam line

Skirt front RS

Band WS

Side seam

Trim gusset seam allowance.

INDEX

Look for these and other *Threads* books at your local bookstore or sewing retailer.

For a catalog of the complete line of *Threads* books and videos, write to The Taunton Press, P. O. Box 5506, Newtown, CT 06470-5506. Or call (800) 888-8286.